T0360644

Václav Trojan
Music Composition in Czech Animated Films

The Focus Animation Series aims to provide unique, accessible content that may not otherwise be published. We allow researchers, academics, and professionals the ability to quickly publish high impact, current literature in the field of animation for a global audience. This series is a fine complement to the existing, robust animation titles available through CRC Press/Focal Press.

Series Editor Giannalberto Bendazzi, currently an independent scholar, is a former Visiting Professor of History of Animation at the Nanyang Technological University in Singapore and a former professor at the Università degli Studi di Milano. We welcome any submissions to help grow the wonderful content we are striving to provide to the animation community: **giannalbertobendazzi@gmail.com**.

Published:

Giannalberto Bendazzi; *Twice the First: Quirino Cristiani and the Animated Feature Film*

Maria Roberta Novielli; *Floating Worlds: A Short History of Japanese Animation*

Cinzia Bottini; *Redesigning Animation United Productions of America*

Rolf Giesen; *Puppetry, Puppet Animation and the Digital Age*

Pamela Taylor Turner; *Infinite Animation: The Life and Work of Adam Beckett*

Forthcoming:

Lina X. Aguirre; *Experimental Animation in Contemporary Latin America*

Václav Trojan
Music Composition in Czech Animated Films

Marco Bellano

CRC Press
Taylor & Francis Group
Boca Raton London New York

CRC Press is an imprint of the
Taylor & Francis Group, an **informa** business
A FOCAL PRESS BOOK

CRC Press
Taylor & Francis Group
6000 Broken Sound Parkway NW, Suite 300
Boca Raton, FL 33487-2742

© 2020 by Taylor & Francis Group, LLC
CRC Press is an imprint of Taylor & Francis Group, an Informa business

No claim to original U.S. Government works

Printed on acid-free paper

International Standard Book Number-13: 978-0-8153-5852-7 (Hardback)

Library of Congress Cataloging-in-Publication Data

Names: Bellano, Marco, author.
Title: Vaclav Trojan : music composition in Czech animated films / Marco Bellano.
Description: Boca Raton : CRC Press, 2019.
Identifiers: LCCN 2019018726 | ISBN 9780815358527 (hardback : alk. paper)
Subjects: LCSH: Animated film music--Czech Republic--History and criticism. | Trojan, Vaclav, 1907-1983--Criticism and interpretation. | Trnka, Jiri, 1912-1969--Criticism and interpretation. | Stop-motion animation films--Czech Republic--History and criticism.
Classification: LCC ML2075 .B43 2019 | DDC 781.5/42092--dc23
LC record available at https://lccn.loc.gov/2019018726

Visit the Taylor & Francis Web site at
http://www.taylorandfrancis.com

and the CRC Press Web site at
http://www.crcpress.com

Jiří Trnka: the most celebrated puppet animation director ever. Václav Trojan: the most significant Czech composer of post–World War II Czechoslovakia. Their work together: a harmonious collaboration between two highly talented people. Period. For about 70 years, the pair's relationship, output, and artistic achievements didn't go beyond these bare-bone appreciations. Marco Bellano, an animation historian and orchestra conductor, eventually fills the gap with this book, and tells both the specialists and the ordinary filmgoers the What, Who, Where, When, and Why of this unique two-man job.

Giannalberto Bendazzi, animation historian

In 2018, Marco Bellano presented a paper on "Jiří Trnka and Václav Trojan's Bajaja" at the Third Chinese Animation Studies Conference in Chengdu. As co-chair of that conference and a Chinese scholar and curator who has long been concerned with the history of European animation, but also as a fan of classical Czech animation, I am very excited to read that research in full. Marco's book reconstructs a historical–cultural space, spanning from Czech art to contemporary music. This approach to animation studies is in tune with the recent scholarship on memory and myth at the cutting edge of interdisciplinary research.

**-Chunning (Maggie) Guo, School of Arts,
Renmin University, China**

To Faranak

Contents

Acknowledgments

THE AUTHOR WISHES TO express his gratitude to Prof. Giannalberto Bendazzi, a mentor and a friend, who generously offered his invaluable support and advice. The research challenges and difficulties that this book posed have largely been overcome because of his help.

Gratitude is here also addressed to another colleague, teacher, and friend: Prof. Alberto Zotti Minici. My academic career in film music and animation studies would not have happened without his continuing backing and trust.

A special thanks to the NFA – National Film Archive in Prague – and especially to Lukas Hanzal and Tomáš Žůrek.

Thank you to George C. Papagiannis, Chief of Media Services at UNESCO, Paris, for allowing research on the film *Proč UNESCO* (*Why UNESCO?*, 1958).

Thanks to Dr. Eva Strusková for her insightful suggestions.

My gratitude goes also to Prof. Massimo Tria, for a frank and friendly dialogue about the Czech language.

About the Author

Marco Bellano, PhD, teaches the history of animation and is a research fellow at the Department of Cultural Heritage of the University of Padua, Italy. He previously taught the history of Italian cinema at the Boston University Study Abroad Padua. Several times he has been guest teacher of film music at the University of Salamanca, Spain. He graduated from the Conservatory of Vicenza in piano and orchestral conducting.

In 2014, the Society for Animation Studies (SAS) presented him with the Norman McLaren-Evelyn Lambart Award for Best Scholarly Article. In 2014, he organized and chaired "Il cinema d'animazione e l'Italia" (Padua, 2014), the first ever Italian academic conference on animation, co-funded by the SAS. He was Chair of the 29th SAS Annual Conference (Padua, 2017).

He is associate editor of the cinema journal *Cabiria* and a member of the scientific board of *Popular Music Research Today* (University of Salamanca) and *Mutual Images Journal*. He collaborates with many orchestras and cultural institutions, including the Palazzetto Bru Zane in Venice.

He wrote the books *Metapartiture. Comporre musica per i film muti* (Cinit, 2007) and *Animazione in cento film* (Le Mani, 2013, with Giovanni Ricci and Marco Vanelli) He is currently writing *Allegro non Troppo: Bruno Bozzetto's Animated Music* (Bloomsbury, 2020). In 2017, he co-edited (with Giannalberto Bendazzi) the final issue of *Animation Journal* issue, on Italian animation.

Introduction

A NIMATION AND MUSIC ARE kindred arts. Their oft-remembered mutual bond, though, should not be taken for granted, or just passively inferred from the existence of a heritage of animated works with a strong musical attitude. There is indeed an impressively long list of animated short films, full-length features, music videos, and video art pieces that set up thoughtful interplays between images, movements, pitches, and rhythms: the renowned examples of the Walt Disney productions, the keen and personal experimentations of Norman McLaren, the wry audiovisual humor of Bruno Bozzetto, and the illuminating metamorphoses of color and sound in Georges Schwizgebel's shorts are among them. Such abundance of musical animation is a consequence of something, more than a cause. A historical fact provides a hint: the affinity between the two expressive fields started to be explicitly addressed well before the late 1920s, when the growing availability of the technology of synchronized sound allowed Disney and others to create a fixed (and even obsessive) counterpoint between animation and its musical score. The pre-cinematographic, hand-drawn animations by Émile Reynaud, presented at the Musée Grévin in Paris from 1892 to 1900, already had piano scores by Gaston Paulin. In comparison, after the debut of the Brothers Lumière's cinématographe in 1895, no film (animated or not) had an especially composed score until 1905. Similarly, the most ancient full-length animated feature still preserved, Lotte Reininger's *Die Abenteur des Prinzen Achmed*

(*The Adventures of Prince Achmed*, 1926), was conceived together with an accompanying symphonic score by Wolfgang Zeller. In the same period, during the European historical avant-garde age, several artists sought the creation of a pure cinema, independent from other arts and, as such, with an absoluteness comparable to that of instrumental music. As they pursued this ideal, they consistently turned to animation, creating abstract silent shorts that were not supposed to be accompanied by music, but that were based on visual equivalents of the musical language. Hans Richter's *Rhythmus 21* (*Rhythm 21*, 1921) ends with something like a crescendo, for example, as "the disparate shapes of the film briefly coalesce into a Mondrian-like spatial grid before decomposing into a field of pure light" (Suchenski 2009). Viking Eggeling, in his *Symphone Diagonale* (*Diagonal Symphony*, 1924), displayed elegant curved shapes to achieve an *"orchestration of time* [...]. He [...] used them according to the musical term *instrument"* (Richter 1952: 81).

What makes animation and music converge is, first of all, a matter of shared core identity, at the level of their basic constituents. The ways artists choose to manipulate such constituents and make them meaningful are similar between the two fields.

The minimal unit, in animation, is the frame (and not the image, as the same image can reappear in distinct frames; for example, when they animate in twos, each image gets repeated for two frames; see Williams 2015: 78). The prime task of an animator is to create meaning out of the reciprocal arrangements of the frames, being in control of each one of them. As Norman McLaren wrote, in animation "what happens between each frame is much more important than what exists on each frame; animation is therefore the art of manipulating the invisible interstices that lie between the frames" (McLaren in Furniss 1998: 5). Among the different meanings that can be elicited by the arrangement of frames, one distinguishes itself for its powerful communicative potential: "not so much the attribution of motion but the attribution of a soul (or a personality) to objects, forms, or shapes (even abstract) that are otherwise lifeless" (Bendazzi 2004: 6).

In the words of a classic scholar of musical aesthetics, in music "the crude material which the composer has to fashion [...] is the entire scale of musical notes" (Hanslick 1974: 66). It would be maybe better to say that the basic constituents are sound events (including also silences). The organization of such events is today much freer than its equivalent in animation. In fact, animation is often used for film or video works, which are technologically bound to a fixed frame rate (for example, 24 frames per second; but there are also other options). Music, instead, can continuously change its time signature and meter, even though more traditional and mainstream compositions do not take advantage of this chance too pervasively. Moreover, music does not only unfold on a single, *horizontal* level (melody), but it also benefits from simultaneous superimpositions between multiple layers of sound (polyphony and harmony). A loose equivalent could be found between musical harmony and the multiple layers that compose an image in hand-drawn cel animation, or the layered approach to key animation in 3D computer graphic works; however, this would probably bring the music-animation parallel too far. In any case, the job of a composer has always been to choose and arrange sound events in a time sequence, in order to achieve an expressive meaning from the relationships between them. The analogy with the act of animating is very strong. Igor Stravinsky observed that the "indispensable and single requirement [of music] is construction. [...] It is precisely this construction, this achieved order, which produces in us a unique emotion having nothing in common with our ordinary sensations and our responses to the impressions of daily life" (Stravinsky 1962: 53). On these premises, Stravinsky then proceeded to make a comparison between music and architecture, which is not a time-based art. A comparison with animation would have been perhaps more insightful but, given his mixed feelings about the use of his Sacre du Printemps in Disney's *Fantasia*, it is understandable why he avoided touching the topic.

Both in animation and musical composition, thus, the aesthetic value derives from a minute and organic time structuring of elementary constituents; the aim is to communicate emotions and meaning. In this respect, they also have a lot in common with language, which is also founded on the organization of minimal cells into larger structures, intended to convey messages; in fact, it is not wrong to identify music and animation as languages of their own.

This grade of affinity between such languages allows them to be coordinated in painstakingly accurate ways that are best exploited when the two roles of animator and composer coincide in a single artist. For example, that was the case of Ferdinando Palermo, an animation director and musician who was a major contributor to the works of the Italian Nino and Toni Pagot; or of Børge Ring, who wrote the music of the shorts he directed. However, this is not a common occurrence; notwithstanding the core similarities, the knowledge and the intensive training needed to achieve mastery in one of the two disciplines are not automatically applicable to the other one – even though fine animators are often in possession of a heightened musical sensibility.

A good alternative to the rare role of the animator-composer is the stable professional association between an author of animation and a trusted composer, or a composer's longstanding practice with a series of stylistically consistent animated works. When a collaboration of this kind goes past its early stages and is consolidated, it easily gives way to solid audiovisual solutions, where music and animations coalesce into inseparable artistic entities. There, it becomes particularly true that the study of the animation can shed light on the musical devices applied by the composer, and the analysis of music can provide a better understanding of its visual counterpart. The critical discourse on those works should thus be fully audiovisual in order to be meaningful: it must equally reference music and animation, with an interdisciplinary approach. In 2005, Daniel Goldmark used this approach to study two of the most outstanding composer-animation ententes in the United States: Carl Stalling at Warner Bros (Goldmark 2005:

10–43), and Scott Bradley's music for MGM's *Tom and Jerry* shorts (Goldmark 2005: 44–76). Another comparable and celebrated pairing was that of Howard Ashman and Alan Menken, for the animated musicals that defined the overall style of the *Disney Reinassance* features in the 1990s. In Japan, the collaboration between Hayao Miyazaki and Joe Hisaishi has been one of the longest and most productive in film history (and not just in animation history), now including ten full-length films and three shorts, with a new feature in the making. Many more couples of artists valorized the music-animation potential, like Maurice Blackburn and Norman McLaren, or Roberto Frattini and Bruno Bozzetto.

The literature on animation and music, however, has mostly overlooked the contribution of the Czech composer Václav Trojan (1907–1983) to the output of the master director and animator Jiří Trnka (1912–1969). Notwithstanding the mainstream success that full-length, stop-motion puppet films are enjoying in the contemporary age, since Tim Burton's *Nightmare Before Christmas* (Henry Selick, 1993) reacquainted mass audiences with their visual aesthetics and paved the way for many Academy Award-nominated and -winning features from studios like Aardman and Laika, Trnka and Trojan remain relatively unsung pioneers in Western countries. Puppet animation, in fact, was Trnka's distinguished specialty; however, he was also well versed and highly original in hand-drawn and paper cut-out animation, and equally so in providing illustrations for children's books. He even directed short films that dramatized still drawings, in an unconscious prefiguration of the photo-roman technique that Chris Marker, with still photographs, was going to use in *La Jetée* (1962).

Trnka's films are today mostly unavailable on home video or on streaming platforms. Only in 2018, a vast (but slightly incomplete) touring retrospective by the Film Society of the Lincoln Center offered to a potentially large audience in the United States, a chance to discover and appreciate his animation in a fitting way.

The most poignant scholarship on Trnka's works is written in Czech; the publications in different languages are sparse.

The majority of the critical contributions were produced during the 1960s and 1970s. A monograph on the director, by Jaroslav Boček, was published in 1963 and translated into English in 1965; in the latter year, another short book about Trnka was written in Spanish by Carlos Fernandez Cuenca. Other essays were part of general works on Czech cinema, like Ernesto G. Laura's *Il film Cecoslovacco* (*The Czech Film*, 1960), in Italian, which featured a major section on animated films by Marie Benešová. More recently (1999), Vlastimil Tetiva wrote in Czech *Jiří Trnka* (1912–1969), a chronological appreciation of the director's life and works. In 2002, Luboš Hlaváček Augustin separately dealt with Trnka's diverse artistic competences in the chapters of his Czech language monography on this topic. A chapter on Czech animation, with a paragraph on Trnka, appeared in Peter Hames's *Czech and Slovak Cinema. Theme and Tradition* (2009). The most recent and authoritative summary on Trnka's artistic relevance appears in Bendazzi's *Animation: A World History* (Bendazzi 2015, 2: 62–67). It is also the only one, among the books that deal principally with Trnka, that expands on Trojan's music in respect to animation, with a specific text box on the topic (Bendazzi 2015, 2: 67–68).

Nonetheless, Trnka retains crucial importance to international stop-motion animation. This is not just because of a mere matter of chronological precedence. Actually, his use of unmoving expressions on the faces of his puppets, and the rendering of their emotions by means of subtle body movements and cinematographic devices like lighting and editing, could even – superficially – seem to be a faux pas, given the virtuosities in facial mimics so common in many puppet films of today, which try to emulate and even surpass the possibilities of the virtual *puppets* of 3D computer graphic features. This assumption would be a severe mistake, though, as facial agility is not essential to the cinematographic effectiveness of puppets; on the contrary, their appeal peaks when they act convincingly and yet their nature as puppets remains in plain view. While the U.S.-dominated mainstream of

Western animation keeps pursuing an *illusion of life*, through a series of animation principles (Thomas and Johnston 1981: 47) intended to conceal the animation process itself, puppets find their communicative strength in appealing to the early fascination of the puppet theater and of the *cinema of attractions*, when the audience was mostly delighted by practical visual effects; people found pleasure in being deceived by something that was clearly a trick, but whose secrets remained unfathomable to the layman. This is why, for example, while the Laika productions embrace a computer graphic-like smoothness, the Aardman plasticine characters are proudly covered in fingerprint marks from their animators, and Wes Anderson used cotton wool instead of computer graphic simulations to render smoke and clouds in *Fantastic Mr. Fox* (2009) and *Isle of Dogs* (2018). This by no means implies giving in to low-quality standards; on the contrary, the expressive power of the foremost stop-motion films stays exactly in a difficult balance between the rough material nature of the puppet and the way it transcends this to become a relatable character, projected into an emotionally relevant narrative by the interplay between the animation, the design, the film language, and the soundtrack. This transcendence, which aptly invites us to use the adjectives *poetic* and *lyrical* – too often otherwise associated with animation in unsubstantial ways – is peculiar to the puppet film, because of the explicit clash between the scope of its emotive vision and the apparent triviality of its players.

However, Trnka was also crucial in defining what a full-length puppet feature is. The transition from the short to the long format, in puppet films, had already been accomplished by European filmmakers before the Second World War (Новый Гулливер, *Novyy Gullivyer*, *The New Gulliver*, Aleksandr Ptuško, 1935, with live-action sequences; *Reinecke Fuchs*, or *Le Roman de Renard*, *The Tale of the Fox*, Ladislas Starewich, first released in Germany in 1937). Trnka reprised this blossoming tradition after the war, and did so to a great extent, by producing a total of five full-length puppet features between 1947 and 1959; no other director has ever equaled this record. Trojan provided music to each one of those features, as well as to the majority of the short films by Trnka, who sometimes collaborated with other Czech composers, and especially with Jan Rychlík (1916–1964).

Just like in Trnka's case, Trojan's stature as a composer is not properly acknowledged outside the Czech Republic and its cultural area. In his country, he was among the foremost musicians and intellectuals of the 20th century, together with his colleagues Bohuslav Martinů (whom Trojan was a little jealous of; Vičar 1989: 147), Jiří Srnka, Zdeněk Liška (a film music specialist), and Jan Novák (who also wrote for Trnka), among others. A first Czech monography about his film music was published in 1958 (Vladimír Bor and Štěpán Lucký, *Trojan – filmová hudba* [*Trojan – Film Music*]). The musicologist Jan Vičar, the most distinguished scholar on Trojan, published in 1989 the monography *Václav Trojan*; an English shortened version of a chapter on the Trojan–Trnka collaboration from that book is part of Vičar's 2005 *Imprints: Essays on Czech Music and Aesthetics*.

Trojan was in possession of an uncommon versatility, as he was able to craft effective chamber miniatures (*Divertimento pro dechové kvinteto* [*Divertimento for Wind Quintet*], 1977) as well as large orchestral works (*Pohádka* [*Fairy Tale*], 1946) and operas (*Kolotoč* [*Merry-Go-Round*], 1936–1940). At the same time, he was an expert of bohemian folk music, which he largely arranged or used as thematic material throughout his whole career (like in the cantata for solos, mixed choir, and orchestra *Naše vlast v písni a tanci* [*Our Country in Song and Dance*], 1936 or in *Z Čech do Moravy* [*From Bohemia to Moravia*] for the same ensemble, 1939). The language of popular dances and songs mingled well with Trojan's musical idiom: only apparently a traditional one, it merges an elegant take on Neoclassicism with an expressive use of dissonances and polytonality, as well as with original research on the expressive value of timbres and sounds. In this last respect, for example, he had a new wooden percussion instrument, the *sobot*, built especially for the score to Trnka's *Staré pověsti česke* (*Old Czech Legends*, 1953) (Vičar 2005: 46).

Trojan's involvement with music for audiovisual entertainment, that is to say, *functional* music, spanned from cinema to TV shows to radio programs that he provided with folk songs arrangements and accompanying pieces for plays. He could be regarded as a pioneer of the music for media in Central Europe. However, he did not consider this field of primary importance for a professional composer; in a not-so-tasteful way, he used to tell his students at the Academy of Performing Arts in Prague (AMU) that being involved with film music was like having a "relationship with dubious women" (Trojan in Vičar 1989: 149). In an address to his potential successors, on his 70th birthday, he stated, "working in film, theatre, and television – it is a beautiful thing, in which one learns a lot. However, one must not succumb to it, because it is one-sided, and it must not become a routine that interrupts a composer in the middle of his most mature choices. I warn against such imprudence" (Trojan in Vičar 1989: 98). This mindset, though, did not prevent him from developing an outstanding narrative sensibility; his pupils and friends remembered how easily he would *tailor* a piece of music to a given dramatic situation, giving to it a perfect and natural aural equivalent. One of his students, Luboš Sluk, recalled that "Trojan explained the dramatic situation, or he said only one word, for example, mom, sat down to the piano and improvised exquisitely" (Sluk in Vičar 1989: 148).

This disposition of his could explain his commitment to writing for films. Trojan completely devoted himself to the uncompromised achievement of the best artistic result, to the point of sacrificing his own health; it happened during the making of Trnka's feature *Bajaja* (*Prince Bajaja*, 1951), when a fire destroyed 1,500 meters of finished film and, because of the subsequent production delay, Trojan was given only a single month to write the music (Vičar 1989: 120). With exhausting effort, he complied. Later, in July 1962, he suffered a heart attack that left him partially disabled; it was probably caused by his lifelong struggles with cinema and stage music deadlines (Vičar 1989: 178).

Trojan's career in film music was largely defined by his partnership with Trnka, in the field of animation; he only seldom wrote for live-action directors, like Bořivoj Zeman (*Byl jednou jeden král* [*Once Upon a Time There Was a King*], 1954) or Václav Krška (*Poslední růže od Casanovy* [*The Last Rose from Casanova*], 1966). He could be then considered an animation specialist, as a film musician; however, he wrote music for an animated short which was not by Trnka only once, in 1946 (*Vodník ve mlýne* [*The Waterman in the Mill*], Josef Vácha). He never returned to animation after Trnka's demise, an event that coincided with the onset of a final stage in Trojan's creative itinerary, when he mostly abandoned music for media and focused on new concert elaborations of precedent scores.

The conscientious dedication Trojan demonstrated in his work with Trnka, notwithstanding his own doubts about the profession of film musician, is likely a sign of the composer's awareness about the affinity between music and animation, and of its huge artistic potential. Moreover, he was also very conscious of the specific musical appeal of puppet animation; when he was working on the film *Sen noci svatojánské* (*A Midsummer Night's Dream*, 1959), he perceived that "the world of puppets required a very specific [musical] rendition" (Vičar 1989: 162). However, that was not just any world of puppets; it was the one by Trnka, an artist with a uniquely strong style and musical sensibility (he played the bagpipes and the guitar himself, as an amateur; Vičar 1989: 108). Trojan's "tailored" approach to functional music, when confronted with such a peculiar and authoritative visual universe, could only result in an extreme specialization, not applicable to other animation productions.

This "very specific rendition" is the object of this book: a short perusal of how and why the animation by Trnka and the music by Trojan interlocked and interacted. In Part One, a few historical coordinates on Czech film music, and on the two authors, will provide context to the audiovisual commentaries of Part Two, about the whole of the Trnka–Trojan production.

The reason behind this investigation is not only a historical one. The assessment of the collaboration between Trojan and Trnka as a landmark in the international development of music-based animation is certainly a desired goal. However, there is also a more general intent, that goes beyond the specific case at issue: to reveal and describe the communicative mechanisms put in motion by the core affinities between music and animation, for the sake of a better understanding of the language of animation as a whole. The complementarity and quality in Trnka and Trojan's approach to this field ease the identification of such mechanisms and provide a set of well-tested and trustworthy examples to the contemporary animation theorist or practitioner.

CHAPTER 1

Czech Animation and Music

Premises and Context

ORIGINS OF CZECH ANIMATION

A large portion of the history of Czech cinema is a matter of puppets, drawings, silhouettes, or cutouts. Films produced with animation techniques in the geographic area centering around Prague started to emerge in the 1920s; actually, what is believed to be the very first Czech animation, the now lost paper cut-out short *Broučci* (*Fireflies*), dates back to 1919. It was directed by an architect, Bohuslav Šula, at the Prague film company Praga-film (Strusková 2013: 24). Its story came from a renowned Czech book for children by Jan Karafiát, *Broučci: pro malé i veliké děti* (*Fireflies: for Little and Big Children*), published in 1876 and, since then, deeply rooted in Bohemian popular culture. Its relevance is testified by its frequent use as a source for new artistic works. A particularly well-received edition of it was printed in 1961; it was illustrated by Jiří Trnka, who had already provided art for a 1941 version of the same text (Benešová et al. 1981: 51). However, even before that, Trnka adapted *Fireflies* into two puppet plays for his own

Wooden Theater in Prague (September 12, 1936) (Kačor, Podhradský, and Mertová 2010: 21). *Fireflies* would also have been Trnka's first animated film: the producer Miloš Havel invited him to turn his 1941 illustrations into a short, requiring the use of mechanical puppets; however, Trnka turned the offer down (Boillat 1974: 488; Strusková 2013: 340–341). In 1942, Václav Trojan wrote incidental music for a theatrical dramatization of Karafiat's text by Jan Disman and Míla Kolář. An animated *Fireflies* by Trnka and Trojan was never made, but it would have made a lot of sense to see such a title in their filmography. It would have responded well to the care in rediscovering and reviving the Czech cultural lore that both that the authors had* and that had apparently been a constant of Czech animation since its very beginning. In fact, on top of its subject matter, the only surviving fragment of Šula's *Fireflies* (a little more than a single frame, reproduced in Strusková 2013: 25) reveals a visual style that homages the detailed and yet caricatural style of old European woodcut prints.

During the 1920s, however, Czech animation languished and, apparently, did not have a meaningful impact on the film production and on the preferences of the audience that, instead, started to be increasingly exposed to American cartoons. Otto Messmer and Pat Sullivan's Felix the Cat, for example, became one of the favorites of the Czech cinemagoers (Benešova in Laura 1960: 168; Strusková 2013: 22, 24). It is difficult to assess what was the average quality of the local animated production during that early age anyway, as many of the films are no longer available. It is known that, in 1920–1921, the architect, painter and actor Ferdinand Fiala, in association with the cameraman, actor and director Svatopluk Innemann, produced three *trickfilms* (live-action films with animated effects) at the Pojafilm studio; Fiala later (1923) created a film featuring a

---

* *Fireflies* was among Trnka's favorite books, because it featured "a world of little people dressed in an old-fashioned way and preserving old costumes, distinguished by their strong moral values" ("l'univers des petites gens vêtues à l'ancienne mode et gardant de vieilles costumes, qui se distinguaient par leurs solides valeurs morales"); in it, "the dream was joined to reality, and the imagination to the real" ("le rêve s'y joignait à la réalité et l'imagination au reel") (Trnka in Benešova et al. 1981: 51).

lonely puppet from a forsaken toy factory that interacted with real actors. The film, that was released three times under different titles (the first one was *Proč se nesměješ, Why Don't You Laugh?*), is now lost (Strusková 2013: 26–28). Other early Czech animations included Antonín Frič's silhouette films *Pohádka o Popelce* (*Cinderella*, 1923) and *Tvrdohlaví milenci* (*The Stubborn Lovers*, 1923). The oldest Czech cartoon preserved is a commercial, *Vizte vše, co tropí dnes kluci dva a jeden pes* (*How Two Boys and a Dog Fool around These Days*, 1925); the author is unknown (Strusková 2013: 28).

The fact that the film industry did not offer a fertile ground to animation is perhaps testified by the fact that several remarkable artists, who were born in territories that are today inside the borders of the Czech Republic, trained and expressed themselves elsewhere: Berthold Bartosch (1893–1968), Peter Eng (1892–1938?), and Walter Trier (1890–1951) (Strusková 2013: 33–34).

Animation had its chance to start writing its chapter in Czech film history only in the following decade, thanks to Hermína Týrlová (1900–1993) and her husband Karel Dodal (1900–1986). They both started off as collaborators with the Urania Theater in Holešovice, participating both in the painting workshop and in a few of the stage plays as extras (Týrlová was a chorus girl). They later joined Elekta Journal, a film production company that, between 1928 and 1929, became the largest of its kind in Prague (Strusková 2013: 39). In the second half of the 1920s, Týrlová and Dodal started to work on hand-drawn animated commercials; they tried to entice the viewers by making explicit use of foreign cartoon stars, like the aforementioned Felix the Cat, or Koko the Clown from the *Out of the Inkwell* series by the Fleischer brothers, slightly disguised as a thin man wearing a straw skimmer.*

---

* The name of the character was Bimbo; this could also have come from the Fleischers, as Bimbo was the anthropomorphic dog in the *Talkartoons* and *Betty Boop* series. However, the character was named for the first time in the 1930 *Talkartoon* episode, "Hot Dog"; the Bimbo films by Dodal were released by Elekta Journal in that same year. It could be that Dodal managed to see "Hot Dog" prior to the release of his commercials; however, Strusková advances that he might have worked on the films between 1927 and 1929 (Strusková 2013: 70). In that case, the use of the name Bimbo would be a mere coincidence.

In 1935, Týrlová watched Ptuško's *The New Gulliver* and was deeply struck by the huge potential of puppets in animated films. As a result of this impression, she prompted her now ex-husband (Dodal remarried to Irena Leschnerová and, with her, he launched in 1933 his own studio, IRE-film) to use puppets in *Tajmeství lucerny* (*The Secret of the Lantern*, 1936), the first Czech animated puppet film – and also, for Týrlová, a big step towards her career as the first Czech specialist of puppet animation, which was going to flourish in the 1940s at the Zlín Studios and span for almost four decades (Bendazzi 2015: 59–60). *The Secret of the Lantern* was a black and white commercial, directed by Dodal with his wife, and animated by Týrlová for the Krása handmade shoes. It parodied the German expressionist cinema,* with a detective-story setting filled by big and ominous shadows that favored the use of silhouettes and animated drawings. Actually, what survives of the film (67 meters out of 70) opens with a long shot of Prague's Wenceslas Square, teeming with flickering lights and hand-drawn speeding cars. Then, we see a caricatural silhouette: when the owner of the shadow is revealed, the transition from the flatness of drawings to the plasticity and chiaroscuro of the puppet is quite a dramatic one. As an overture to the country's most original film tradition, it was perfectly fitting: it established a clear distinction between the frenetic hand-drawn aesthetics, at that time associated by the audience with the foreign U.S. cartoons (somehow hinted in the opening cityscape, which, despite being a stylization of a Prague sight, feels stereotypically American) (Figure 1.1) and the totally different feeling exuded by the limited movements and fixed facial expressions of Czech puppets. It was as if animation shifted gears and started to appeal to a completely different sensibility; the extent of this divide was evidenced by Trnka, when he confessed that he distanced himself from animated drawings

---

* It seems to use Fritz Lang as a main reference; apart from shadows and camera angles, the *videophone* featured in a sequence is likely inspired by the device Joh Fredersen uses to talk with the master of the workers in *Metropolis* (1927).

FIGURE 1.1   Prague in the opening shot of *Tajmeství lucerny* (*The Secret of the Lantern*, Irena Dodalová, Karel Dodal, 1936). (From Národní filmový archiv/National Film Archive [NFA], Prague. With permission.)

because he believed they have "a grotesque quality, which is their very essence. The drawing moves restlessly, it wriggles, it swarms about, and it must do so because as soon as it stops, it dies; it turns flat and still" (Trnka quoted by Benešova in Laura 1960: 138).*

WHY PUPPETS? THE CZECH PUPPET THEATER TRADITION

Such a transition towards the quieter and three-dimensional world of puppets, however, was also eased by the Czech familiarity with an entertainment vogue which was already strong with a long-standing tradition in Bohemia at that point: the puppet theater, and in particular the *loutkové divadlo*, which used stringed and articulated figures put in motion by an offstage puppeteer. Other

---

* "[Quello che mi mette soggezione nei disegni animati è il loro] carattere grottesco, che è la loro stessa essenza. Il disegno si muove senza posa, guizza e brulica, e deve brulicare perché al momento stesso in cui si·ferma, muore; diventa piatto e inerte."

forms of puppet theater, like the *bramborové divadlo* (*potato theater*), based on hand puppets, were present but less successful and influential (Bogatyrёv 1980: 43). The passing of the baton between the *loutkové divadlo* and its cinematic reinvention took place in three short films whose protagonists were former stars of the puppet stages. *The Secret of the Lantern*, in fact, was not the first Czech film featuring puppets: it was the first one to be mostly based on animated puppets. Before it, puppets were seen on film in *Spejblův případ* (*Spejbl's Case*, Josef Skupa, 1930), *Spejblovo filmové opojení* (*Spejbl's Fascination with Film*, Josef Skupa, 1931), and *Všudybylovo dobrodružství* (*The Adventures of a Ubiquitous Fellow*, Irena Dodalová, Karel Dodal, 1936). They all starred a couple of characters whose names were highly familiar to the Czech popular audiences: Spejbl and Hurvínek. They were the protagonists of the stage shows and radio plays by Josef Skupa (1892–1957), the foremost Czech puppeteer between the two world wars.

Skupa, a native of Strakonice, became in 1917 a leading personality at the Loutkové divadlo Feriálních osad (Holiday Camp Puppet Theater – a summer camp for poor children) in Plzeň (Pilsen), the same city where Jiří Trnka was born. In fact, Skupa became Trnka's junior-high art teacher; quite soon, Trnka was hired as his assistant and puppet carver (Bendazzi 2015: 62). Slowly but steadily, Skupa made himself a name by reviving the Czech puppet tradition that, between the 18th and 19th centuries, had a decisive role in promoting awareness about the cultural identity of Bohemia during the Czech National Revival (Laura 1960: 132). For example, the traveling puppeteer Matěj Kopecký (1775–1847), whose descendants mastered puppetry for six generations, championed the use of Czech language in his plays against the directions of the government, who prescribed German for the theatrical practice: Kopecký claimed that it was not his fault if his puppets did not speak anything but Czech (Bogatyrёv 1980: 46). For this reason, sometimes restrictive orders were issued against puppeteers who were considered outlaws together with bandits and gypsies, as happened in Prague in 1802 (McCormick and Pratasik 1998: 21). Anyway, in the years of the Austro-Hungarian domination, Kopecký's puppets managed to spread the ideas of the Enlightenment and of national identity through straightforward humor and a simple language. Skupa took a similar role in the aftermath of the First World War by having his puppets stage political revues (like *Kaspar's Cabaret*, from 1916), to satirize the Austro-Hungarian Empire (Boček 1965: 14). When the state of Czechoslovakia was established in 1918, he continued to pursue an approach to puppetry which did not shy away from appealing to an adult audience too, as opposed to the trend that, between the 19th and 20th centuries, devalued the puppet theater as something for children only. This had probably happened because of the unequal distribution of talent in the families of puppeteers: the sons could master the techniques, but maybe they were not as convincing and committed as their fathers (Benešova in Laura 1960: 132). Skupa did not come from such a family tradition, so he was freer to reinvent puppetry on his own while respecting its heritage. Most notably, he acknowledged that the power of Czech puppets stayed in their iconicity and straightforwardness. The traditional plays revolved around recurring types of characters; a habit that could be loosely compared to the premises of the Italian *Commedia dell'arte*. The most successful type, since the late Baroque, was the *Pimprle*, later known as *Kašpárek*: a simpleton with a subversive attitude which symbolized the latent qualities of the average man; in that, he was a very relatable character. Skupa revisited the *Pimprle* in 1919 with Spejbl, a middle-aged bald fellow who wore a tailcoat with clogs and white gloves. He was not from any social class in particular, so as to facilitate the identification of the audience (Jirásek 2015: 203). At first, Spejbl co-starred with Kašpárek and his role was intended as comic relief for children: sometimes his clothes had pieces of smelly cheese attached to them in order to instigate a wild reaction from the puppetmaster's dog (Jirásek 2015: 203). Only after 1922, Skupa gave to Spejbl a distinct personality and voice. He also gave him a son, Hurvínek, in 1926, to substitute for Kašpárek and establish a completely new stage couple. A creation of the puppet carver Gustav Nosek (Jirásek 2015: 204–205), Hurvínek shared with Spejbl his overall appearance as well as the fixed facial expression that was integral to the Czech puppet aesthetics: a universal and recognizable mask, with large, inquisitive eyes sporting small pupils.

Skupa's national relevance consolidated in 1930, when he established his own touring ensemble, based in Plzeň; the adventures of Spejbl and Hurvínek on stage, however, started to be paralleled by a different series of shows, made for the most modern mass-communication technologies of the time. Skupa widened his audience by having his plays broadcasted through radio revues and gramophone records (Strusková 2013: 106). A choice of this kind, completely focused on the verbal (and musical) side of the puppet theater, provides a good hint about the extent of the character's fame; their voices alone were enough to guarantee an enthusiastic audience, thanks to Skupa's extraordinary acting abilities: "Skupa's vocal range [went] from a sonorous bass, through a baritone, tenor, to a childish falsetto. Besides, he was able to differentiate each of them into several independent registers and was able to play up to six roles within a show in such a convincing way that the audience would not recognize that these were the performances of one person" (Jirásek 2015: 215–216). This also testifies to how relevant sound was to the puppet theater; the shows were often completed by music in the form of parodic performances of the latest light songs.*

From Stage to Screen

Skupa's confidence in the aural appeal of his plays contributed to his skeptical attitude towards cinema. In a 1941 letter to Vladimír Pošusta of the Zdar-film company that wanted to produce a puppet feature, Skupa, who by that time had already seen the three

---

* One of those songs was *Tři strážníci*, (*The Three Policemen*), performed during the revue *Utrpení Spejbla i Syna Jeho*, (*The Suffering of Spejbl and of His Very Son*), in September 1929 (Jirásek 2015: 221). A revue Trnka wrote for the Holiday Camp Puppet Theater in autumn 1935, *The Merman*, featured "popular songs current at the time, taken from the repertoire of Marlene Dietrich" (Boček 1965: 27).

aforementioned shorts featuring Spejbl and Hurvínek, evidenced a few reasons behind his disbelief in cinema:

> I am again returning to the reasons why I keep being reluctant to make a puppet picture. Something like Gulliver, which cost [*sic*] loads of money and the army of people working on it had lots of time and all technology available, can never be our guideline. Other films with puppets acting directly through motion mechanisms require limited space. Strings cannot be prolonged endlessly. A puppet can only act close to the background because someone must always stand behind it, pulling the strings. If we film a theater as it is performed on the puppet stage, it won't be a film but instead a filmed theater and the critics will tear us to shreds. If we solve everything by filmmaking means, a roughly carved figure all over the screen won't look good; it will come out as a monster. And the close-ups can be even worse if the puppet lacks facial gestures.

> (SKUPA IN STRUSKOVÁ 2013: 339)

Trnka would later demonstrate that, with a carefully conceived facial design, a puppet with a fixed expression could convey complex emotions by means of animation and cinematography, and thus be able to star in a full-length feature; the three early shorts with Spejbl and Hurvínek, instead, had been too limited in running time and technique to show that Skupa's needs could be somehow met. In fact, he consented to their making only after having turned down many offers from different companies; afterwards, he concluded that "shooting was extremely time consuming, [...] it collided with his work in theatre and [...] it even did not pay off financially" (Strusková 2013: 106).

In addition to that, it seems that Skupa did not completely trust the animation process that would have been able to bring to life

puppets on the big screen, the so-called stop-motion animation.*
The first Spejbl short, *Spejbl's Case*, was actually not an animation
at all: the puppets moved thanks to visible strings so it was a case
of a puppeteer's performance caught on film and edited, more
than a piece of puppet animation. The same can be said about
Spejbl's Fascination with Film† (Figure 1.2), even though, in this
case, Skupa provided a script that explicitly acknowledged cinema and its language. The story itself was a satire of the cinema
industry: it focused on Spejbl and his attempt to start a film production, soon to be targeted by a scheming swindler; some wise
words from Hurvínek end Spejbl's troubles. The story also featured a Radiojournal broadcast. On top of that, for the first time
the screenplay contained vast annotations by Skupa, intended to
prompt the cinematographer (Jan Stalich) to use close-ups, pan-
oramic camera movements, fade-ins and film editing (Strusková
2013: 108). However, the final film made little of such suggestions, as it mostly showed the stringed puppets through wide
shots and fixed camera angles. Notwithstanding this, the film was

---

* The name *stop-motion* conventionally identifies all those types of animation based on
pictures of physical objects whose aspect can be modified by posing them in different
configurations; every pose of such objects is modified (and lost forever) after each shot.
In animated drawings, for example, the poses (the drawings) are instead preserved. The
general principles of animation can be thus applied to a multitude of physical objects:
puppets, clay figurines, paper cutouts, sand, and even real people, in the stop-motion
variant known as pixilation. Stop-motion is sometimes called a *frame by frame* technique;
however, it is not recommendable to use this expression as it is misleading. In fact, it is not
true that each picture of a posed object becomes a frame of the final film, instead, a picture could be repeated in two, or even three different frames. This is a possibility of animation in general; it is called animating *in twos*, or *in threes*. The one-to-one correspondence
between pictures and frames happens only when the animator is working *in ones*. So the
frame by frame expression does not sufficiently identify the stop-motion process; instead,
it indicates that, in *every kind* of animation, the author is in control of the relationships
between the single frames.

† When stop-motion animation became common practice in Czech cinema, the puppets
on the big screen lost their strings for good as they could be photographed one pose at a
time, without any need for a live-action puppeteer off screen. However, they were given
back their strings (and they were, again, shot in live-action) in 1959, when Emil Radok,
a puppet theater scholar, created his film *Doktor Faust*, based on one of Kopecký's
plays. It was a singular hybrid between a documentary and a historical reconstruction
of an old puppet show; it was considered a "formalist" effort by critics, and the experi-
ment was never attempted again. (Benešova in Laura 1960: 165).

FIGURE 1.2   Spejbl and Hurvínek in *Spejblovo filmové opojení* (*Spejbl's Fascination with Film*, Josef Skupa, 1931). (From Národní filmový archiv/National Film Archive [NFA], Prague. With permission.)

announced as "the first Czech 100% spoken puppet film," and Strusková argued that it might be considered "the first Czech puppet film" (Strusková 2013: 108), as opposed to *Spejbl's Case* that was "just a filmed puppet sketch." *Spejbl's Fascination with Film* is surely more than a sketch, but, again, there is no puppet animation in it. The historical relevance of this short stays precisely in its carefully constructed soundtrack. What Skupa actually achieved for the first time in his country was a cinematographic management of dialogues, effects, and music in a film that, for the most part, did not feature live actors.*

Sound and Music in Early Puppet Films

The sound of *Spejbl's Fascination with Film* is so important also because its key plot points revolve around radio broadcasts. This

---

* It opens with a live-action prologue featuring the leading Czech comedian Jindřich Plachta, aka Ms Acetylene, a close friend of Skupa.

remarkable centrality of the radio, both as an object and a sound source, invited people to suspect that the film was intended as a disguised commercial for the Radiojournal company; actually, a month before the premiere, Skupa had a frame from the upcoming film printed in the Radiojournal magazine and presented the work with a slightly altered title: *Spejbl's Fascination with Sound* (Strusková 2013: 108). In fact, at that stage of his career, Skupa was about to invest more energies into his radio shows; at the same time, Radiojournal made an offer to Skupa and to the Dodals' IRE-film to shoot a commercial featuring Spejbl and Hurvínek, which was to become *The Adventures of a Ubiquitous Fellow*.

Spejbl's Fascination with Film has the typical soundtrack of an early sound film: dialogues, effects, and music are quite rigidly juxtaposed in order to avoid overlapping layers of sound that would have been poorly rendered by low-fidelity, monaural cinema speakers. However, for the first time, the short dares to entrust a couple of puppets with a showstopping moment: the interpretation of a song. Spejbl and Hurvínek are in charge of singing *Handkiss, Missus*, the main theme of the film.* Their *spoken* singing, in a *Sprechstimme* style, is not as remarkable as the way the puppeteer accompanies every accent and emotion of the song with appropriate and synchronized body movements which compensate for the total lack of facial expressions or lip movements. The performance is surely rigid and quite poor from a cinematographic point of view (the camera is motionless, and the shot is unbalanced, as it shows the full figures Spejbl and Hurvínek on the right side of a furnished room). However, the mutual interaction between subtle movements and the musical phrasing set an important premise to the later exploration of the visual matching between puppets and human singing voices in Trnka's films. The song itself, anyway, maybe also thanks to the charisma of Skupa's voice acting,

---

* The music was composed by Rudolf Kubín, whose name, in the opening titles, appears immediately after that of Skupa: this might be intended to stress the importance Skupa gave to sound and music in this production.

became widely popular and enjoyed a record release by Ultraphon (Strusková 2013: 108). This kind of film music marketing, based on actual excerpts from the soundtracks or on new arrangements of favorite musical pieces, would later become a distinguishing trait of the Czech animation panorama. Trojan's composition for Trnka (and their concert versions) often enjoyed a parallel success as bestselling records.

A similar destiny was reserved for a selection from Jaroslav Ježek's music for *The Adventures of a Ubiquitous Fellow*, issued by Radiojournal in order to promote the film internationally (Strusková 2013: 124). Ježek's manuscript shows that Dodal and his collaborators must have, in a timely manner, provided the composer with precise guidelines about the needed musical atmospheres which gave way to a twelve-part subdivision of the composition, bearing descriptive titles like *Hurvínek on the Moon, Falling, Organ, Light Bulbs* and so on (Strusková 2013: 117). However, the music was not composed by looking at the animation; on the contrary, the final synchronization was achieved by means of post-production adjustments and selections by Bedřich Kerten. In this, the production strategy seemed to be still under the influence of silent film music practices, heavily based on compilations of musical *moods*, fitted to the finished film by means of arrangements or live improvisations.

Moreover, the musical style adopted by Ježek (a mixture of American swing and European salon music in the vein of many *fin de siècle* light pieces for small orchestras), suggests that Czech puppet animation had still to develop its own musical language. Ježek directly applied to Dodal's film his influential experience at the avant-garde and anti-fascist Liberated Theater (Osvobozené divadlo) in Prague, where he conducted the orchestra and collaborated on the revues and films of the renowned playwrights and comedians Jan Werich (1905–1980) and Jiří Voskovec (1905–1981). Their efforts consolidated the fame of the Liberated as the most remarkable and original theater company in the country between 1927–1939 (Jirásek 2015: 221). So, Ježek's renowned style was surely a welcomed and authoritative addition to Dodal's film and, as such, it needed to stay recognizable. The choice of Ježek was fitting also because Skupa was one of his colleagues at the Liberated Theater, and Ježek had already almost provided Spejbl and Hurvínek with accompanying music for the revue *Vest Pocket Varieté*, an "hour-long show, combined with film," that however was never finalized due to conflicts with the Prague City Council (Pavel Grym in Jirásek 2015: 221–222). Ježek's take on jazz was to become appreciated even in New York, where the composer worked until his death in 1942 (Vičar 2005: 17). Even though his influence on 20th-century Czech music was large, in the end, Ježek did not develop a musical approach specific to animated films or puppet shows.

The Adventures of a Ubiquitous Fellow, moreover, is not a puppet film: it is mostly made of animated drawings that give Hurvínek a new, two-dimensional design. This is why the original name of the character is never mentioned, and his new incarnation is instead identified as Všudybylovo, the *ubiquitous fellow* of the title. The animation is sometimes alternated with footage from pre-existing documentaries about the radio waves; the short is, in fact, an educational piece intended to inform the audience on the technical principles of radio broadcasting.

The prologue to the short, however, was interpreted by Hurvínek in his more familiar puppet persona (Figure 1.3). The shifting nature of the character, from a puppet to a flat drawing, maybe explains why the authors called him *ubiquitous*; anyway, that introduction finally lets Hurvínek move on screen without any strings attached, marking thus the beginning of Czech stop-motion puppet animation.

The stop-motion sequence shows Hurvínek on stage in front of a microphone and under a spotlight. After a very short musical cue, we hear an invisible audience clapping. The puppet starts a monologue. Even though the animation is sometimes not perfectly paced, the build of the puppet is not fully optimized for the stop-motion treatment yet, and the lighting feels quite generic, the movements are expressive and convincing.

FIGURE 1.3 Hurvínek in *Všudybylovo dobrodružství* (*The Adventures of a Ubiquitous Fellow*, Irena Dodalová, Karel Dodal, 1936). (From Národní filmový archiv/National Film Archive [NFA], Prague. With permission.)

This prologue was also the first time when the name of Jiří Trnka was associated with a stop-motion animated puppet. He was the designer and carver of this version of Hurvínek, following the explicit requirements made by Skupa himself. At that time, Trnka had just graduated from the School of Applied Arts and was already in charge of the set designs and the overall keeping of the Wooden Theater (Dřevěné divadlo) in Prague. It is unclear whether Trnka participated in the animation or not, but it is likely that he must have worked in close contact with Dodal and his crew. The sequence, anyway, does not create any interaction between music and animation, as it is exclusively based on Hurvínek's monologue.

When *The Secret of the Lantern* brought on screen a whole cast of animated puppets, making them the main attraction of its story, it also proposed a musical treatment intended to compensate for the limits of the puppet acting, while also enhancing their distinct appeal. The music, by Kerten (the same artist who adapted Ježek's music to *The Adventures of a Ubiquitous Fellow*), responds principally to two preliminary narrative requirements: the noir/detective story atmosphere of the short, and its nature of a commercial, thus in need of a catchy tune to be easily remembered by the potential buyers. In the first part, a *film noir* style prevails; starting from the opening titles, Kerten creates a menacing and ebullient series of fragmentary cues, mostly dominated by dissonant chords of the brass and woodwinds sections. The American feeling of the images is somehow reinforced by momentary melodic passages given to a solo trumpet, playing with the *wah-wah* effect (obtained by opening and closing the trumpet bell with a mute) which was often heard in swing or jazz pieces of the time. Sometimes a wind sound dialogues with the music, as well as an obsessive ticking whose cause is being investigated by the detective: it will be revealed that it is caused by a company of merry shoemakers, intent on nailing shoe soles inside of an oversized lantern (a joke on *Lucerna passage*, one of the entrances to an intricate system of passages that runs under the Art Nouveau Lucerna Palace in Prague; the advertised shoemaking company was based in one of those Lucerna passages). At that point, the musical style changes, and the shoemakers sing together a chorus with a folk flavor with evident expressive *ritardandos* that precede energetic reprises of the pristine tempo: a typical performance convention of popular tunes from Central and Eastern Europe that had a "rather free, speech-like rhythm" (Rosenblum 1994: 52). The puppets are animated according with the musical phrasing, signaled by synchronized movements of their heads and arms, and also by a few steps of square dance. So the first part of the short is exclusively about augmenting the images with a musical *mood* without any synchronic association between sound and movements; on the contrary, the *folk* song triggers visible correspondences between the main articulations of the music (accents and *ritardandos*) and the character animation: it is a dance-like accompaniment.* Both those basic strategies would later appear in the works by Trnka and Trojan, even if not so rigidly separated, and in a more elaborated audiovisual context. Also, the schematic alternance between music and sound effects would be abandoned, not only because of the developments in the sound film technology, but to take advantage of a different conception of the soundtrack with the music solely in charge of rendering every sound event, including noises.

SMETANA AND THE PUPPET THEATER: A CASE STUDY

It seems natural to find signs of emotional and rhythmic correspondences between music and visual elements in the earliest Czech puppet films because of their direct connections with the Czech puppet theater. It is known that, in Skupa's plays, "each puppet in the musical scenes was carefully timed in performance, and in character, according to the ensemble in which it appeared" (Eric Hudson in Jirásek 2015: 224).

Music had a relevant role in the historical puppet theater tradition (Bogatyrëv 1980: 108) even though not many written scores have been preserved. Improvisation and compilations of existing music were more common than formal musical composition also because "travelling companies, if they did not have their own musicians, would generally hire them locally" (McCormick and Pratasik 1998: 156). Sometimes, the music was provided by amateurs from the family of puppeteers that was staging the show (McCormick and Pratasik 1998: 209). In this context, impromptu compilations of favorites from the popular or classical repertoire

---

* Commentary and accompaniment are the two basic audiovisual functions identified by the film music theorist Sergio Miceli. The first one is a relationship created by an accordance (or a provocative discordance) between the mood of the images and of the music; it is based on the emotive content only. Accompaniment, instead, is a rhythmic function: it appears when there is some degree of correspondence between the pacing of the music and of the movements on screen. See Miceli 2009: 631–642.

were a fast and effective way to leave an impact on the audience, while not requiring the skills of professional musicians. Songs had a special place in this practice: their notoriety favored a stronger engagement in the show by sometimes having the audience sing along (McCormick and Pratasik 1998: 157), and they also enhanced the most important sound feature in puppet plays, which, as already said about Skupa's performances, was the voice of the puppeteer. While the puppet films by Trnka were mostly driven by musical pantomime, puppet plays heavily relied on the vocal performance of the puppeteer who enacted multiple parts by altering his voice according to the personality of the character. Such caricatural manipulation reduced the expressive gap between the presence of a human voice and the motionless, deformed face of the puppet (Bogatyrëv 1980: 107). Dialogues were extensive and probably much more important than music; just like in the earliest puppet film featuring Spejbl and Hurvínek, the authors cared about making the verbal content more interesting and surprising by using a plethora of word plays and figures of speech, like oxymorons, metatheses, synonyms, homonyms, metaphors, and iterations (Bogatyrëv 1980: 50–76).

Nonetheless, the fame of puppet theater favored a series of musical contributions from relevant Czech composers who (like Ježek) agreed to write for the miniature stage. The participation of Trojan and other major 20th century composers in the repertory of Czech puppet animation was a continuation of this trend that was inaugurated by Bedřich Smetana (1824–1884), the "founding father" of the Czech musical language (Dohnalová 2005: 24).

In 1862 and 1863, Smetana wrote two overtures for puppet plays by Kopecký: *Doktor Faust* and *Oldřich a Božena* (*Oldřich and Božena*). They were both created for the Umělecká Beseda (Society of Arts), a society for Czech artists whose music section was presided by Smetana himself. Those short orchestral pieces, printed only in 1945, were intended as part of the End-of-Year celebrations at the Society. It is not known if, or how, the actions of the puppets were supposed to be choreographed to the music.

However, the structure and emotional tone of the overtures provide valuable hints to understand what kind of musical strategies were at work during the performances of the puppeteers.

The 1862 *Doktor Faust* was initially "to be presented with neither players nor puppets, but Beseda members imitating the stiff movements of Kopecký's marionettes," even though Smetana wanted it to have a "serious side" (Large 1970: 128). In 1863, *Oldřich and Božena* tried to make fun of "the itinerant bands of musicians whom he possibly heard in his childhood" (Large 1970: 128). The writing of *Oldřich and Božena* is in fact blatantly conventional, for the sake of comedy. Its rigidly separated sections are replete with obsessive repetition of banal harmonic successions, standard accompaniment patterns, and band-like fanfares. *Doktor Faust*, instead, had a different approach to comedy based on quirkiness and dramatic impact. This is evident even by looking at its scoring that calls for two horns, bass trombone, triangle, bass drum, strings, and piano; a quite unusual choice, compared to the two clarinets, two horns, trumpet, timpani, and strings of *Oldřich and Božena*. *Doktor Faust* consists of a very unexpected succession of episodes; each one of them, rather than being a completely separate module, prepares the ground for the next one, from an emotional point of view. The dramatic pattern is mostly the following, a very strong emotion is clearly instated by the music, only to get surprisingly contradicted by the next section. The unity of the discourse is guaranteed by the use of a single thematic cell, a four-note motif that is basically an arpeggio derived from the triad built on the tonic note of the tonality in use; a C, in this case. This is a very simple, and apparently trivial, thematic choice. As such, it is incredibly versatile, as it can be easily used as a familiar signal while combined with more complex musical features; such a use of basic motifs is also at the core of Trojan's music for Trnka. The triad on the tonic note, in a given tonality, is the one that more straightforwardly tells the ear what the harmonic context is, and that immediately communicates to the listener the culturally codified emotional *flavor* of that tonality. For example, the triad

C-E-G instantly reveals the tonality of C major and its associated feeling of positivity, luminosity, and stability. On the contrary, C-E flat-G marks a C minor context, which the European culture (especially after Ludwig van Beethoven's *Symphony no. 5 op. 67*) attaches to despair and turmoil. Smetana first introduces his motif as C-G-E flat-D, with the extra D serving as an embellishing tone to get back to the pristine C and then circularly repeat the motto. So, the overture opens in C minor, though it ends in C major with an emotionally "uplifting" modulation that was quite common, as a dramatic device, in 19th century music (even the aforementioned Beethoven's *5th* used it); however, Smetana exacerbates the mood whiplash by creating humorous contrasts in the various sections. *Doktor Faust* opens with a C minor series of ostinatos carved out of the ascending or descending repetition of two notes in different registers. Each ostinato ends in a tearing chord after a short crescendo. This aggressive and ominous introduction is followed by a four-part* string fugato: an episode where an instrument proposes a subject (the four-note motif, that gets introduced here) and then others join in imitation. The mood gets more severe, because of the reference to the fugue – a learned composition technique from the past. It leads to an orchestral *tutti*, where the motif peaks in intensity. However, it is a matter of only a few seconds: suddenly, the piano plays a melancholic solo on the main theme. This is the first time the listener becomes aware of this instrument as it previously only reinforced, unnoticed, the orchestral texture during the peaks of intensity. It is just the first of a number of *effects* that Smetana introduces by playing with musical timbres and expectations; for example, after a second *tutti*, a new unlikely soloist debuts: a trombone, an instrument that very rarely had solo parts in 19th century music. Its stentorian *voice* seems to prepare for a tragedy; instead, Smetana suddenly introduces a bouncy dance variation on the motto, now

---

* However, only three parts at a time play together. When the fourth and higher part enters, the lowest one (the cello) stops playing.

in C major, enlightened by the shimmering sound of the triangle. After a few more stormy and dissonant chords, again in the parallel tonality of C minor, this dance episode returns, paving the way to a swirling final peroration of the motif. Before that, however, Smetana unleashes one more surprise: while the piano plays gloomy scales in its lower register, the strings are asked to hit their music stands with the bow. Such shrill percussive effect had already been experimented with by Gioachino Rossini in his *Ouverture* to the opera *Il signor Bruschino* (1813); however, it was not of frequent use, and its sudden appearance was surely likely to leave the listener wondering about the origin of that sound.

The overall conception of *Doktor Faust* reveals a communicative strategy sustained by fast-paced emotive contrasts and surprising effects. It might be excessive to say that *Doktor Faust* should be considered a model for music in Czech puppet plays; however, the principle of continuous emotive variation that holds its structure together (and that appears throughout the many parodistic short sections of *Oldřich and Božena* too) seems to be an appropriate counterbalance to the stiffness and facial stillness of the puppets, and as such it would have been profitably used during the shows. Musical variety in puppet plays, after all, was also a necessary consequence of the compilations of favorite pieces that were used as incidental music. The final effect might had not been far from the one seen in *The Secret of the Lantern*, with its sudden mood change in the middle. Moreover, such a dramatic setup seemed to mirror the attitude of dialogues in puppet plays: to take the audience off-guard, with compelling puns and figures of speech.

The emotive strategy that Smetana applied to his puppet overtures also implied a connection with the folk musical traditions of Central and Eastern Europe, not in the harmonic or melodic language, but in the pacing of the musical discourse. Just like the chorus of the shoemakers in *The Secret of the Lantern* featured frequent tempo changes, *Doktor Faust* and *Oldřich and Božena* fragmented their flow with radical mood contrasts. This might be, then, a Dumka approach. *Dumka* is a word derived from the Ukrainian language and borrowed (with slightly different spellings) by several Slavic languages, including Czech; it derived from *duma*, "a Slavic (specifically Ukrainian) epic ballad [...] generally thoughtful or melancholic in character" (Randel 1978: 148). The basic meaning is *to think*; a related Czech expression, *dumat o něčem*, indicates the action to think deeply about something. *Dumka*, a diminutive, came to designate the musical compositions connected with these ballads. Classical composers, and especially Slavic ones, connotated this genre as "a type of instrumental music involving sudden changes from melancholy to exuberance" (Randel 1978: 148).

The soundscape of the *loutkové divadlo* was thus a quite lively one, replete with compelling contrasts of voices, effects, and moods; it was also well connected with the Czech musical folklore by means of performances of popular songs and indirect references to the Dumka genre. The first Czech puppet films perpetuated those basic traits, even though at a smaller scale, because of artistic, technological and financial limits. However, those films also started to contaminate musical tradition of the puppet theater with international film music, as happened in the *film noir* opening sequence of *The Secret of the Lantern*. Those processes of conservation and hybridization in music for Czech puppet animation would have become more evident and fully productive in the 1940s, when Trojan and Trnka started their collaboration.

CHAPTER 2

Jiří Trnka

Early Career and Relationship with Music

Jiří Trnka [...] worked easily, quickly, and always with a well-developed artistic concept. He devoted his entire life to art, relaxing only once a week by drinking wine on [a] Saturday evening. He had a well-ordered mind and paid close attention to the smallest details of his work. [...] Trnka was a *big boss* surrounded in the film studio by high-caliber people – and was always able to get the best out of them. He was selfish but able to provide excellent conditions to ensure good results from his collaborators. He was cool and reserved as a person, and sober in creative expression as well because of the nature of the artistic material he used.

(VIČAR 2005: 41)

Tᴴɪꜱ ᴘᴏʀᴛʀᴀɪᴛ ᴏꜰ Tʀɴᴋᴀ, part of Vičar's short essay on the artistic partnership between the director and Trojan – the only study in English on this topic – is one of the best succinct accounts on the artist's personality. It refrains from veiling the relevant information with the excess of superlatives often found in texts about Trnka, and it also acknowledges his collaborators; in fact, Trnka was not an animator, but an illustrator, an engraver, a sculptor, a designer, a storyboard artist, and a director.

Maybe as a consequence of his reserved personality, the available biographical essays about Trnka* are just quite generic chronologies of his puppet shows, illustrated books, and films, sometimes spiced up with trivia regarding the director's imposing appearance, his enigmatic deep scar on the right cheek (which might as well be a natural facial feature and not the consequence of a wound), his serious and occasionally brusque temperament, as well as his – reported – penchant for drinking. No source has inquired into the reasons behind his artistic choices and psychological traits with a verifiable historical methodology.† In-depth research on Trnka's biography is among the major scholarly contributions that are still missing in the field of Animation Studies.

Such research would be beyond the scope of this book; this is why this chapter focuses only on basic and verified facts from the first part of Trnka's biography, until his debut as a film director. As Trnka also started to encounter and appreciate music at a professional level in his early years, the discourse will expand on this side of his artistic training.

The rest of Trnka's career will be commented on during the discussion of the films by him and Trojan. The director's biography

---

* See the Introduction.
† Film historian Eva Strusková, in a personal email communication to the author (September 10, 2018), reported that there has been no serious archival research on Trnka's biography by any Czech scholar yet; Boček's book was written at a time when state archives were not accessible, and so he had to rely on secondary sources and accounts from relatives of the director.

as a whole, anyway, could tentatively be subdivided into three main periods. The first one (1912–1945) covers the years of his training and of his first successes in the puppet theater and as an illustrator; it is closed by Trnka's participation in the establishment of the Prague animation studio *Bratři v triku* [*The Brothers in Shirts*, but also *The Brother of Tricks*: a clever Czech pun by Trnka himself (Bendazzi 2015: 58)]. This period coincided with dramatic historical circumstances. It encompassed two world wars; the proclamation of the Czechoslovak Republic on November 14, 1918; the attempts of Prime Minister Tomáš Garrigue Masaryk (elected in 1918, 1920, 1927, and 1934) to establish a democratic system, giving voice to the needs of all the different ethnic groups; the fall of this system after the dismemberment of the Republic into a Naziphile Slovakia, ruled by the Catholic priest Jozef Tiso, and the areas of Bohemia and Moravia, turned into a protectorate by the invading Nazi Germany; the creation of an exiled Czechoslovak government, first in Paris and then in London, guided by Edvard Beneš; and the Liberation and the return of Beneš and of the Republic.

The second period of Trnka's career spanned from 1945 to 1957: he created most of his animated films during those years until a hiatus that occurred from 1957 to 1959 when the artist returned to illustration. The social and political situation of the country induced a growing disillusionment in Trnka: a new form of dictatorship appeared, under the control of the local Communist Party and of the USSR. Notwithstanding appearances, liberal democracy was suppressed (all the political parties were grouped into the National Front that served the Communist Party only). In 1948, Czechoslovakia became a socialist state.

In 1959, Trnka returned to animation with his last full-length feature, *A Midsummer Night's Dream*. He would have only authored a few more shorts until 1965, when his last work, *Ruka* (*The Hand*) was released. Such late works were imbued with sour and at times cumbersome satire, resonant with his depression and pessimism about freedom of expression in his country.

The 1968 Prague Spring* (Caccamo, Helan, and Tria 2011: 15), fueled by a liberalization attempt helmed by the new First Secretary of the Communist Party, Alexander Dubček, did little to give Trnka new hopes: USSR troops invaded Czechoslovakia on the night of August 20–21 to prevent any further distancing from the political and social status quo. In 1969, Dubček was expelled from the Party and replaced; the Party itself was purged of its liberal members. Trnka died on December 30, 1969. However, the seeds planted by the Prague Spring would bear fruit after the Velvet Revolution of 1989 when democracy was restored and the state was subdivided (in 1993) into the Czech Republic and Slovakia.

TRNKA THE PUPPETEER

Trnka was born in Pilsen (now Plzeň) on February 24, 1912, an important city in West Bohemia, famous for its beer-brewing facilities. His family had been one of artisans and craftsmen: while his father, Rudolf, was a plumber,† his mother, Růžena, was a dressmaker, who created Jiří's first toys out of rags (Boček 1965: 13). She recorded her memories of Jiří and his younger brother Rudolf in a diary, published in 1972 (Trnkova 1972). Trnka's grandmother, Madlena Rohbergerová, is said to have been an earthenware painter, as well as a toy and doll maker (Boček 1965: 13; Cuenca 1965: 11 holds that Trnka's grandparents were woodcarvers who specialized in figurines from the popular culture).

Skupa's Holiday Camp Theater in Pilsen soon became one of the main interests of Trnka as a child, who was demonstrating also a few early signs of talent in drawing and toymaking (Cuenca 1965: 11; Boček 1965: 13; Boillat 1974: 478). He had also been developing

---

* Even if the expression "Prague Spring" is more common, "Czechoslovak Spring" is preferable to remark the contribution of the whole state to the events, and not just of the capital (Sylvie Richterová in Caccamo, Helan, and Tria 2011: 15).

† Benešova et al. 1981: 12 acknowledge the existence of uncertainty about Trnka's father's job: some sources say that he was a plumber, others identify him as a locksmith. Strusková clarified that he was a plumber (klempíř), and that the confusion is due to translation errors (personal email communication to the author, September 10, 2018).

an interest in the circus, which seemed to leave an even stronger impression on him than the puppet theater (Trnkova in Boillat 1974: 478).

The Holiday Camp Theater was first run by Skupa in 1916, when Trnka was four. In 1923 (according to Benešova et al. 1981: 12; Cuenca 1965: 11 claims that this happened in 1921) Trnka won an art competition run by Skupa himself at the Theater, with a drawing of the puppet Kašpárek. Trnka then entered the local junior high school where Skupa was an art teacher (Boillat 1974: 481); he was hired by his teacher as a puppet carver and scene designer in 1927. After a period he had to drop out of school because of the dire economic circumstances of his family (his father's business went bankrupt), and to train as first a pastry cook, and then as a locksmith (Boček 1965: 17).

The first puppets that Trnka built were already in possession of a few distinguished traits, destined to remain in his more mature creations. The characters created by his mentor Skupa, Spejbl, and Hurvínek, had a purposely weird appearance with rounded heads, spread apart and wide-open eyes (like those of a fish), and mouse-like ears: this enhanced their comedic attitude. Trnka instead used a softer approach to caricature, as he was interested in a wider range of narrative genres. Among the characters he assembled during his training – a selection of protagonists from literary works he enjoyed, by William Shakespeare, Miguel de Cervantes, Maurice Maeterlinck, and Julius Zeyer, not destined for any show in particular, but meant for practice only and to be exhibited – there was also Puck, the mischievous spirit from *A Midsummer Night's Dream* (Benešova et al. 1981: 12). Like his later incarnation in Trnka's 1959 full-length feature, this Puck had an anatomically consistent body with a carefully sculpted face; however, this face was mouthless, and the realistically-shaped eyes were big and dark, with no visible pupils. Even in those first trials, Trnka had already identified an expressive terseness of great emotional potential: the most important feature of the puppet is the face, but it suggests emotions more than describes them, like an archaic mask (Boillat called them *mask-puppets*;* Boillat 1974: 479). To achieve this, the mouth is kept small (or omitted) and posed without any evident reference to an inner state (one notable exception is Švejk's candid smile in the three shorts of the series *Dobrý voják Švejk* [*The Good Soldier Švejk*], 1955). However, more importantly, even when the mouth is a bit larger because of character design requirements (like in the Sancho Panza puppet seen in Boček 1965: 22), the eyes retain primary importance in emotional communication. The gaze of the characters is not pointed towards a precise direction: when they have irises, they seem to look into a distance, lost in deep thought. The big irises (or the total blacking of the eye) help in conveying this indetermination of the gaze; sometimes the eyelids are half-closed or completely shut. This treatment of faces is also present in Trnka's paintings and drawings which he provided to books for children and satirical magazines from 1929. On this topic, one of Trnka, as a director's, most esteemed collaborators of Trnka, and a director himself, Břetislav Pojar, wrote "I often noticed Trnka, while he was painting his actors' heads. He always gave their eyes an undefined look. By merely turning their heads, or by a change in lighting, they gained smiling or unhappy or dreamy expressions. This gave one the impression that the puppet hid more than it showed, and that its wooden heart harboured even more" (Pojar in Bendazzi 2015: 67). As this trait appeared so early in Trnka's artistic production, it looks like it was not developed to meet the acting needs of puppets with a fixed expression in stop-motion animated cinema. It was, instead, an integral part of the gentle sense of indetermination that drove his style in every field: "a starting-point of fantasy, rather than a means to direct the imagination. His pictures were intended to be the first link in a chain of associations" (Boček 1965: 31). Puppet theater, paintings, illustrations, and, later, films, for Trnka were all part of a unitary creative impulse: this is one important reason why, in Czech

---

* "Marionnettes-masques."

animation, "there is no visible hiatus between puppet theater and animated puppet cinema" (Bendazzi 2015: 63).

After a new suggestion made by Skupa (who also persuaded the family of his young disciple), from 1928 Trnka perfected his artistic abilities at the School of Applied Arts in Prague; up until 1935, he was trained by renowned teachers like Jaroslav Benda who taught Trnka engraving and employed him in his own atelier. Trnka made a living by taking commissions from Skupa and providing illustrations to magazines, while staying in a flat with his brother who had moved to Prague before Jiří.

While Trnka completed his education, his work started to reach a wider audience. In 1929, Skupa sent a few of Trnka's puppets (some from plays, and some from the *training* ones) to an exhibition in Prague (Boillat 1974: 482; Benešova et al. 1981: 12 say that this happened in 1931); similarly, some puppets were displayed in Paris (Benešova et al. 1981: 12). In 1931, an exhibition of his paintings was held in Stockholm, and a Goethe exhibition in Leipzig featured carvings by Trnka illustrating the ballad *Der Totentanz* (Boček 1965: 23; Benešova et al. 1981: 12, and Cuenca 1965: 11 claim that this happened in 1932). More than by having his work exhibited, however, Trnka preferred to reach his public with puppet performances; moreover, notwithstanding his success as an illustrator, he always preferred sculpture to drawing (Boillat 1974: 478–479). Right after his graduation, in 1935, his main concern was the reopening of the Holiday Camp Theater, which Skupa had left after he decided to become a touring professional puppeteer in 1930 (Jirásek 2015: 222). Trnka co-wrote (with the bandleader Jaroslav Kuncman, a close collaborator of Skupa), designed, and staged *Master of the Sea* (Bendazzi 2015: 63), a parody of seafaring adventure stories. The success of the performance, which was also represented in Prague, persuaded Trnka to establish and manage a puppet theater of his own. The Wooden Theater opened on September 12, 1936, at the Rococo Hall in Prague: Trnka proposed a play from Karafiat's *Fireflies*, titled *Mezi broučky* (*Among the Fireflies*) (Kačor, Podhradský, and Mertová 2010: 21). Even though the shows he staged were initially greeted with enthusiasm, as in the case of *Vasil a medvěd* (*Basil and the Bear*), adapted from a fairy tale by Josef Menzel (1901–1975), the Wooden Theater did not last more than a year: the shows were mostly intended for children, and the audience dropped in Spring 1937, after a new take on Karafiat's book written, again, with Kuncman (*Christmas at the Fireflies*) (Boček 1965: 28). However, the plays of the Wooden Theater were destined to influence some later films: the narrative world of Menzel, which Trnka explored also in the shows *Míša Kulička* (*Misha the Bear*, 1936) and *Pan Eustach, pes a sultán* (*Mr. Eustachius, the Dog and the Sultan*, 1937), returned in the puppets Trnka designed for the short *Misha the Bear* (Karel Baroch, Eduard Hofman 1947), as well as in *Veselý cirkus* (*The Merry Circus*, Jiří Trnka, 1951), that merged suggestions from *Basil and the Bear* with Trnka's childhood love for the circus. Trnka also revisited Menzel's works in his book illustrations (*Míša Kulička v rodném lese* [*Bruin Furryball in His Forest Home*], 1939), right after his efforts with the puppet theater were definitely over (he would never work as a stage puppeteer again), and he went back to drawing and painting. A notable book Trnka illustrated in this period was *Zuzanka objevuje svět* (*Susan Discovers the World*, 1940), about the early life experiences of the daughter he had with Helena Chvojková (the writer of the book), whom he married in 1936. In that same year, Trnka had his first encounter with cinema when Skupa asked him to create a Hurvínek puppet destined to be animated in the short *The Adventures of a Ubiquitous Fellow* (see Chapter 1).

TRNKA THE ILLUSTRATOR, PAINTER, AND DESIGNER

From 1938 to 1945, Trnka divided his energies between many different jobs, including toymaking and the organization of more exhibitions. Illustrations remained central in his creative life; he also dedicated himself to painting, consolidating a style now distinguished by dynamic contrasts between bulky and simply modeled volumes (probably inspired by the physical features of puppets) and mysterious atmospheres, mostly evoked by the use of light that was not naturalistic, but a dramatic element, often emanating from unexpected places and creating haunting ambiguities in the definition of spaces. An oil painting by Trnka from this period, *Betlém* (*Bethlehem*), portrays a nativity scene set among snowy hills and cliffs; the incongruous proportions of the puppet-like characters and of the background elements suggest a miniature stage, maybe a diorama. However, the brightness of the snow and the glow emanating from the inside of the hut where baby Jesus is (unseen, beyond the little crowd in adoration) create multiple areas of chiaroscuro, each one with their own, independent visual rhythm (for example, the backlight effects in the area of the nativity scene contrast with the frontal lighting of the group of characters on the right). Each area is visually consistent: the eye is thus invited to explore the canvas one section at a time, more than appreciating it as a single unit. This creates pacing in the delivery of the painting: an organization of time that might be a hint of the rhythmic sensibility that Trnka later applied to cinema. Bethlehem was actually used by Trnka as a reference for his first puppet animation, with the same theme and title, destined to become the concluding segment of the full-length feature *Špaliček* (*The Czech Year*, 1947).

Apart from the intense commitment to illustrated books for children (in 1940–1945 he illustrated more than 32 different titles; Benešova et al. 1981: 14), the new decade offered Trnka several chances to lend his abilities to a different kind of stage production. During the Second World War, Skupa was persecuted and then arrested by the Gestapo; his first post-war foreign tour happened only in 1947 (Jirásek 2015: 223). During that period, Trnka accepted a series of commissions from Jiří Frejka (1904–1952), a stage director and producer from the Národní divadlo (the National Theater) in Prague; he had met him at one of his own many exhibitions (Boček 1965: 42). Trnka was hired as a scene and sometime costume designer for new productions of plays by, among others, Carlo Goldoni

(*Il bugiardo* [*The Liar*], retitled as *Benátská maškaráda* [*Venetian Masquerade*], 1941),* William Shakespeare (*The Winter's Tale*, 1941),† and Titus Maccius Plautus (Pseudolus, *The Liar*, 1942).‡ The latter play exposed Trnka to the talent of the comedian Ladislav Pešek, whose pantomimic abilities left a longstanding impression on the future filmmaker and were possibly used as inspiration for the acting of characters like the jester in *Prince Bajaja* and Puck in *A Midsummer's Night Dream* (Boillat 1974: 487). Trnka would continue to provide designs to the National Theater until 1943; he later drew costumes for one more production, the historical drama *Drahomíra a její synové* (*Drahomír and Her Sons*, 1959),§ by Josef Kajetán Tyl, a key cultural figure in the 19th century Czech National Revival. The theme of this play was in accordance with the interest for Czech folklore and traditions that Trnka developed over the years and that he expressed in films like *The Czech Year* or *Staré pověsti české* (*Old Czech Legends*, 1953). According to Boček (1965: 48), this inclination of Trnka's was born out of an experience related to the National Theater, that is the scene design for a staging of *Libuše*, an opera by Bedřich Smetana that opened the National Theater itself in 1881, and that is one of the foremost products of the Czech National Revival and of Czech national music. On that occasion, Trnka not only had his first artistically conscious encounter with Bohemian myths and legends, but also learned the language of musical theater. Soon afterward, he would meet Václav Trojan and his music.

---

* http://archiv.narodni-divadlo.cz/default.aspx?jz=cs&dk=Inscenace.aspx&sz=0&ic=14 48&abc=0&pn=256affcc-f002-2000-15af-c913k3315dpc Accessed September 21, 2018.

† http://archiv.narodni-divadlo.cz/default.aspx?jz=cs&dk=Inscenace.aspx&sz=0&ic= 3206&abc=0&pn=256affcc-f002-2000-15af-c913k3315dpc Accessed Semptember 21, 2018.

‡ http://archiv.narodni-divadlo.cz/default.aspx?jz=cs&dk=Inscenace.aspx&sz=0&ic=28 09&abc=0&pn=256affcc-f002-2000-15af-c913k3315dpc Accessed September 21, 2018.

§ http://archiv.narodni-divadlo.cz/default.aspx?jz=cs&dk=Inscenace.aspx&sz=0&ic=37 93&abc=0&pn=256affcc-f002-2000-15af-c913k3315dpc Accessed September 21, 2018.

TRNKA AND MUSIC

The scene design job for *Libuše* was assigned in 1939, after a national public competition, that Trnka won (Bendazzi 2015: 63). However, Trnka's work never reached the stage because the opera was called off after the German invasion (Benešova et al. 1981: 14) as it was considered dangerous to offer shows that could favor an upsurge of patriotic feelings (Boček 1965: 48). Nonetheless, Trnka considered the contents of the opera deeply: Libuše, a mythical queen of Bohemia, protagonist of one of the most important legends about the birth of the Czech nation, would have returned in puppet form in *Old Czech Legends*.

The work on *Libuše* might also have reinforced Trnka's understanding of the importance of music to Czech folklore and its tales. As already reported (see the Introduction), Trnka himself learnt how to play a traditional instrument like the bagpipe, and also a bit of guitar. Vičar (1989: 108) reported that, on one occasion, at a winery of the order of the Piarists, Trnka competed with gypsy musicians to see who knew the most folk songs,. He was probably already confident in his knowledge of music and of the song heritage of his country when he first met Vacláv Trojan in 1941.

At the time, Trnka was 29 while Trojan was 34; Trojan was music director and program manager for the Prague Radio. The two future collaborators were at the villa of a shared acquaintance of theirs, the surgeon Antonín Kostelecký. Their encounter was described by the composer as follows:

> I remember that I and Trnka sat at the table facing each other and, although we were so close, we did not talk for a long time, out of mutual respect and shyness. Some wine helped in loosening our tongues. We had a lot to talk about, and our conversation continued at the piano. We felt like we were people of a similar kind. Or even from the same nest, because we were both born in the city of Plzeň. At the piano, we mainly talked about art. This was

where the premises for our long-term cooperation were created.

(VIČAR 1989: 84)* (FIGURE 2.1)

Even though no precise information is available about the details of Trnka's musical education and the extent of his competence on this matter, the strong intellectual connection he achieved with Trojan, and the work method he later established to express the cinematographic potential of his partner's compositions at their best, are indirect proof "that Trnka had a deeply refined sense of music" (Vičar 2005: 41). First of all, the partnership between the two of them would not have worked if not on the premises of a

FIGURE 2.1   Trojan and Trnka. (From Národní filmový archiv/National Film Archive [NFA], Prague. With permission.)

---

* "Pamatuji se, že jsme byli s Trnkou umístěni u stolu proti sobě, a ačkoli jsme měli k sobě tak blízko, dlouho jsme na sebe nepromluvili pro samou vzájemnou úctu, a proto i ostych. Na pomoc přišlo na stůl víno, které nám rozvázalo jazyky. Měli jsme si hodně co říci a naše rozmluva pokračovala u klavíru. Cítili jsme, že jsme lidé podobného druhu. Dokonce z jednoho hnízda, poněvadž jsme se oba narodili v Plzni. U toho klavíru jsme si hlavně tiše povídali o umění. Tady se vytvořily základy pro naši dlouholetou spolupráci."

shared core of knowledge and sensibility: Trojan and Trnka were in fact profoundly different in their personalities and approaches to their professions. According to Vičar, Trnka "had a well-ordered mind and paid close attention to the smallest details of his work. [...] He was selfish, [...] cool and reserved as a person, and sober in creative expression [...]." Trojan, instead, "was rather emotional and impulsive, often composing under stress and at times upsetting Trnka by doing nothing. [...] [He] completely lacked egotism. [...] While Trnka was said to be a sad *lyricist*, Trojan was said to be a *merry* one" (Vičar 2005: 41).

On the other hand, the work method they adopted could only be used by someone with a mature understanding of musical aesthetics and communicative strategies as it was not based on predetermined rules, but on intuition, trial, and error.

The method was divided into three stages. The first one was mostly guided by Trnka, who used to initiate a film project by sharing with Trojan ideas, sketches, and plot elements. The ensuing discussion between the two was meant to detail the expressive goals through mutual suggestions about the narrative content, visual solutions, and so on. Trnka was reportedly very open to considering Trojan's opinions even when they meant a detour from his intentions: the composer recalled that, on many occasions, Trnka revised his directorial conception after hearing Trojan play for him some musical sketch that did not follow the original plan (Vičar 1989: 108).

The second stage was led by Trojan: in accordance with a rough outline of the time divisions and expressive qualities of the story, he proceeded to create a score. He usually had a whole year while Trnka kept working on directing the film and his animators. This stage was concluded by the recording of the music at the Prague studio in Smečkách street; Trojan kept editing details in the music even during the recording sessions with the help of the sound engineer Jan Zavadil.

The third stage was the one that better demonstrated how precise was Trnka's understanding of music and of its dramatic qualities.

Trnka listened to the music, played from soft gramophone records, and adapted the time proportions of the film, as well as the acting of the puppets, to what he heard (Vičar 1989: 109).

Further evidence of Trnka's musical culture is the learned references to Czech composers or musical pieces that appeared in some of his writings and works. In a letter quoted by Vičar (1989: 103–106), Trnka expressed his concerns over an artistic crisis Trojan underwent during the production of *Old Czech Legends*; his point was, quite provocatively, that any impasse can be overcome if an artist is truly talented, hard-working, and self-disciplined. To back his argument, Trnka gave examples such as Leoš Janáček, who said to his mentor and choirmaster Pavel Křížkovský that a composer can recover from an apparent loss of ideas by purifying himself from the "superficial noise on the soul"[*] (Vičar 1989: 103). Trnka then referenced Bedřich Smetana, and how he kept working even though he was deaf and lamented his illness a great deal.

Hints about Trnka's musical knowledge exist also in his films. His second short as a director, the hand-drawn animated short *Zvířátka a Petrovští* (*The Animals and the Bandits*, 1946), was not simply a variation on the *Town Musicians of Bremen* fairy tale: Trnka based it on the version of the Brothers Grimm's story that appears in Act 5 of the 1908 ballet *Z pohádky do pohádky* (From Fairy Tale to Fairy Tale), by Czech composer Oskar Nedbal. The film was thus set to an adaptation (by Trojan) of Nedbal's music.[†]

Similarly, as argued by Petr Janeček (Česálková 2017: 117), the feature *The Czech Year* seems to have borrowed formal and structural aspects from the 1933 ballet *Špalíček* by Bohuslav Martinů rather than from the most popular text that bore the same title, the 1906 and 1912 collections of folk materials *Špalíček národních*

---

[*] "Povrchního šumu na duši."

[†] The ballet was reprised at the National Theater from September 24, 1939, to June 25, 1944; Trnka was working there in the same period, so he might have known that staging, with scenes designed by Josef Matěj Gottlieb. http://archiv.narodni-divadlo. cz/default.aspx?jz=cs&dk=Inscenace.aspx&ic=2660&pn=256affcc-f002-2000-15af-c913k3315dpc&sz=0&zz=OPR&fo=000 Accessed February 5, 2019.

písní a říkadel by Mikoláš Aleš. Quite meaningfully Trnka himself, in the letter where he addressed Trojan's artistic crisis, compared Aleš to Smetana, a musician, saying that the former never reached the stature of the latter (Vičar 1989: 105).

BROTHERS, TRICKS, SHIRTS, AND FILMS

Trnka's meeting with Trojan in 1941 was arguably the last major event that prepared the ground for the artist's professional debut as a director of animated films. His commitments as an illustrator, painter, and designer continued until 1945, the year of the Prague uprising in the last days of the Second World War in Europe (May 5), and of the subsequent liberation of Czechoslovakia by the Red Army (May 9). That marked the beginning of the Soviet influence over the nation, and of the cultural reconstruction after the Nazi oppression. Even though the new political situation was still going to pose heavy limits to the freedom of expression (as Trnka himself would point out in his late and sourly satirical films), the new government started to promote arts and creativity. Meaningfully, cinema was the first Czechoslovakian industry to be nationalized, on August 11, 1945: it was not seen as a mere profit means, but as a resource of creative, cultural, and national interest (Casiraghi 1951: 14).

A studio specializing in film tricks, often involving animation techniques, had been active in Prague since 1935: the AFIT – Ateliér Filmových Triků (Film Tricks Studio). There, Vladimír Novotný and Josef Vácha, with the collaboration of Jaroslav Jílovec and Josef Říha, operated a single camera to produce visual tricks and subtleties; they also built miniatures intended as substitutes for expensive sets (Hurtová 2010: III). During the Nazi occupation of Bohemia and Moravia, the AFIT was controlled by the German investor Josef Pfister. Renamed AFIT-Zeichenfilmproduktion, it was appointed to produce animated films by the German government and started its new activity on October 21, 1940. The artistic director was Richard Dillenz, an architect of Austrian origins; most of the artists were ex-students who could not afford college taxes. Among them there were Vácha, Richard Bláha, Stanislav

Látal, Karel Štrébl, Čeněk Duba, and Jiří Brdečka: many of them have become outstanding names in the history of Czech animation, as well as close collaborators of Trnka.

After an unfinished attempt at a feature-length film (*Orpheus a Euridika*, *Orpheus and Euridyce*), the Studio produced the unsuccessful *Zauberlehrling* (*The Sorcerer's Apprentice*): Dillenz was thus removed from his role and unofficially substituted by Zdeněk Reimann. In 1943, the Prag-Film Company acquired the Studio and made it a special department dedicated to animation, now named Zeichenfilmabteilung der Prag-Film A.G. However, it remained under the control of the German Ministry of Propaganda. The film *Hochzeit im Korallenmeer* (*Wedding in the Coral Sea*) was produced in 1944; in the same year, the caricaturist Horst von Möllendorf became artistic director; his style was said to be a mixture of distasteful Berlin humor and Disney clichés (Hořejši and Struska 1969: 8).

Pfister and Dillenz briefly returned to guide the Studio in July 1944; however, the Prag-Film animation department was definitively shut down on September 1, 1944, due to the war.

After the liberation, the AFIT group of ex-college students approached Trnka in search of a new artistic director to restart their studio. Trnka had never been in contact with the AFIT leaders, but he knew several animators from that facility, including Brdečka. The invitation to Trnka came from him, Eduard Hofman and some other colleagues of theirs (Bendazzi 2015: 63). Trnka gave them a positive reply even though he was aware of his lack of experience in the field (Boillat 1974: 488). He then opened a new and groundbreaking phase in his artistic career by directing a hand-drawn animated short, initially intended to be a puppet film: *Zasadil dědek řepu* (*Grandpa Planted a Beet*, 1945), that also inaugurated the activity of the renovated studio, now known as *Bratři v Triku*: the *Brothers of Tricks* or *Brothers in Shirts*, as seen in the animated logo by Zdeněk Miler. The music of that first film was by Trojan.

CHAPTER 3

Václav Trojan's Music

A Stylistic Outline

O UTSIDE OF THE CZECH territory, it is usually quite uncommon to find a music connoisseur, or even a professional
musician, who is familiar with the name and works of Václav
Trojan. This, however, does not indicate a marginality of Trojan
as a composer; on the contrary, he is held by scholars to be one of
"the most notable stage and film music composers of the time"
(Dohnalová 2005: 38), and "one of the most prominent 20th-cen-
tury Czech traditionalists" (Vičar 2005: 37). The reason why his
fame barely crossed the Czech border is not related to the quality and relevance of his artistic output; it has instead to do with
a wider condition that affected many of his colleagues. Vičar
articulated this problem in five concurrent causes: the lack of an
international festival for Czech composers; a traditional orienta-
tion of Czech music in the 20th century that did not fit into the
international preference for avant-garde; the limited connections
between Czech culture and the rest of the world after 1948, because
of political circumstances; the fact Czech music was almost exclusively printed by domestic publishers; and too few contacts with

the Western European and North American centers that orientated the worldwide trends of culture (Vičar 2005: 33–35). In fact, the only Czech composers who reached international fame after 1948 are the ones whose careers significantly developed outside of their country, like Martinů.

Trojan never worked abroad; his professional life was prominently centered around Prague. A portion of his output, his film music, had however several chances to reach international audiences during his lifetime, as Trnka's films were featured in several European festivals. The most acclaim usually went to the director, and the name of the composer did not circulate as much; nonetheless, the outstanding role of the music in those films was understood and commended by critics. Two positive reviews of the score for *The Emperor's Nightingale*, for example, appeared in *Film Music Notes*, the official publication of the National Film Music Council in New York, in May 1951 (Hepner 1951; Deke 1951). In 1962, the CIDALC (Comité International pour la Diffusion des Arts et des Lettres par le Cinéma) gave Trojan three accolades at its festival in Valencia, Spain: the Golden Mercury Award for the music of *A Midsummer Night's Dream*, a prize for *The Czech Year*, and a lifetime achievement award (Vičar 2005: 40).

In his own country, Trojan had actually an artistic relevance that extended well beyond the area of film music. He wrote almost 400 works, encompassing chamber pieces, symphonic suites, and concertos, orchestrations, songs, ballets, incidental music, an opera, and dance and folk compositions.* Even though his music was often narrative and intended to complement a theatrical or cinematographic play, and his professional life was tightly bound to mass-media communication (he was music director and program manager for Prague Radio from 1937 to 1945), he believed that being exclusively committed to such creative grounds would hinder the development of a mature musical sensibility (see the Introduction). Thus, he consistently widened the scope of his

---

* The complete catalog of Trojan's music was compiled by Vičar (1989: 333–379).

artistic research during his life, and he reworked his stage and cinematic music into multiple concert suites, as if to prove its inherent versatility.

Trojan's style reached its first peak of maturity and stability in 1936, when the composer seriously embraced a continuing interest of his in the folklore of his country. The folk repertoire had been his first prolonged exposure to music during his childhood in the Czech countryside of Plzeň, from 1907 to 1922; in fact, he was born in a family with no musicians in it. Coincidentally, his father was involved with a visual profession not far from cinema: he was the village photographer. Trojan further developed his inclination for music when attending school at the Knights of the Cross Monastery in Prague in 1919–1920, where he sang in the choir; in this respect he was also influenced by Josef Klazar, the choirmaster of the main church of the pilgrimage town of Stará Boleslav, on the outskirts of Prague (Vičar 2005: 38).

Trojan then entered the Prague Conservatory to study composition. His teachers were Jaroslav Křička and Vítězslav Novák. Křička (1882–1969), as choirmaster, was another figure who might have contributed in developing Trojan's taste in vocal music, as well as his inclination for musical training for children; Křička was, in fact, a specialist of such repertoire (Dohnalová 2005: 36). Novák (1870–1949) is regarded as one of the leading Czech composers of the first half of the 20th century. A pupil of Antonín Dvořák, at the end of the 19th century he steered his style towards a personal interpretation of Moravian and Slovak folk music, resulting in numerous song cycles or pieces with a folk theme, like the *Slovácká suita* (*Slovak Suite*) for a small orchestra of 1903 (Dohnalová 2005: 34). Novák might have had a significant role in consolidating Trojan's own take on musical folklore.

After his graduation, though, Trojan did not immediately pursue a traditionalist and folkloristic approach to composition. From 1929 to 1936 he made a living by playing the violin and the piano in cafés, and also by accepting jobs as an arranger or composer of modernist, jazz, and contemporary dance music. In

1936 he abandoned any attempt at modernism; he abandoned his youthful interest in the music of Arnold Schönberg and turned to neofolklorism and neoclassicism. The following year he joined Radio Prague.

Vičar (2005: 38–39) suggested that Trojan's decisive turn towards a traditional style, with a high communicative potential, was also functional to his understanding of the social and political situation of his country at the time. His revival and reinterpretation of the musical heritage of his country was an artistic reply to the occupation of Czechoslovakia by Nazis in 1938. In order for this message to reach as many people as possible, he decided on a style that was familiar to the masses and he agreed to lend his music to popular media, such as films and radio broadcasts. The feelings that guided Trojan's traditional choice were actually shared by many of his colleagues and mentors. The overall Czech musical style of the first half of the 20th century was inclined to traditionalism: "this was a defensive nationalism of a small nation striving to save its very existence and the values it had created" (Kouba and Volek, n.d.: 59). The tendency to appeal to the audience through the use of music in popular media was also common: "during the major part of its historical existence Czech music was tied to fulfilling various social functions; autonomous aesthetic viewpoints were asserted rather exceptionally" (Kouba and Volek, n.d.: 59).

In the end, anyway, Trojan's mature style was not completely alien to the major trends of European music; even though the composer was peculiarly consistent in his use of Czech folk materials, his language had relations with Igor Stravinsky's neoclassicism, and his instrumentation style could be compared with that of Maurice Ravel (Vičar 2005: 39).

After 1936, the four main features that oriented Trojan's inspiration, and that need to be considered when approaching his music, were thus Czech folklore, neoclassicism, high communicative functionality, and attention to children and themes of childhood. The latter is particularly specific of Trojan, and probably a natural consequence of his concern to reach a broad audience (as well as a result of his studies with Křička). However, Trojan did not write educational music for young musicians in the fashion of Robert Schumann's *Album für die Jugend op. 68* (1848) or of Béla Bartók's *Mikrokosmos Sz. 107* (1926–1939). Instead, he wrote music for a young audience, that sometimes included the presence of child singers (as it happened in many of his scores for Trnka); the intent, though, was not to teach about the orchestra, like in Sergej Prokofiev's *Петя и волк* (*Petya i volk, Peter and the Wolf, op 67*, 1936), or Benjamin Britten's *The Young Person's Guide to the Orchestra op. 34* (1946), but to entertain young listeners with a language they could relate to, balancing a personal and refined musical writing with a light and straightforward attitude. It was often narrative music, intended for the stage; the most pertinent tradition to cite here is that of children's operas like Engelbert Humperdinck's *Hänsel und Gretel* (1893) or Cesar Cui's *Красная шапочка* (*Krasnaja šapočka, Little Red Riding Hood*, 1912), or also Paul Hindemith's *Wir bauen eine Stadt* (*Let's Build a Town*, 1930) and *The Little Sweep op. 45*, part of Britten's *Let's Make an Opera!* (1949).

The only opera Trojan ever wrote was an opera for children, composed between 1936 and 1940: *Kolotoč* (*Merry-Go-Round*, 1941). The generous proportions of the six-act work, and the effort Trojan put into writing it, are a strong statement in respect of the relevance of children themes to Trojan's music. *Merry-Go-Round* is a concretization of the aesthetic turn Trojan took in 1936; its traditional appeal had critics accuse it of formalism (Vičar 1989: 59), but it is actually "the top expression of Trojan's modernism" (Vičar 1989: 64),* even though it used the language of neoclassicism. In perspective, *Merry-Go-Round* is also a prelude and preparation to the music Trojan was going to write for Trnka's films, in respect to style, target audience (children), and functional role, being a complement to narration. As such, *Merry-Go-Round*

---

* "Kolotoč je ze stylového hlediska vrcholným výrazem Trojanova modernismu."

could be used as a reference in order to put Trojan's choices in film music writing in context.

Various circumstances, in 1936, invited Trojan to tackle an opera for children. A two-month collaboration with the Pražské dětské divadlo (Prague Children's Theater) and its director, the actress Mila Mellanova, allowed Trojan to approach stage music for the first time, as well as to have a better understanding of quality musical entertainment for children. Afterward, his first commissioned jobs for radio broadcasts came from the children's choir of Jan Kühn; for example, he was asked to produce adaptations of traditional children songs for the so-called school radio (Vičar 1989: 50).

Such songs were played during shows hosted by Marie Charousová-Gardavská, a renowned author of books for children. She was the one who introduced Trojan to Kühn; she was also going to write the libretto for *Merry-Go-Round*.

This libretto is actually considered the weakest point of the opera (the composer was aware of that, as he personally tried to improve it, by changing its structure and verses; Vičar 1989: 62); however, its content was in tune with Trojan's need for straightforward communication. *Merry-Go-Round* tells the story of four children that ride on different seats of the titular attraction: a car, a horse, a plane, and a duck. As the Moon decides to grant the children's wishes, the seats come alive and lead the children to four different fantasy adventures, until they return to reality and to the merry-go-round. One of the adventures, the one told in the fifth act, has a curious connection with cinema; the little girl riding the duck is brought to the United States, where she becomes a great film star. Soon, however, her duties become suffocating, and she misses the times when she was free to play. The Moon ultimately takes her away from the crowd of people who demand her attention. There are, however, other elements of *Merry-Go-Round* that, more poignantly, appear as a testing ground for Trojan's future film music aesthetics.

The narrative structure of the opera, first of all, offered to Trojan a challenge similar to that he was to face in Trnka's *The Czech Year* and *Old Czech Legends*: writing music for a thematically unitary work, subdivided into short independent episodes. The necessity to single out each part with a musical identity, while keeping a sense of cohesion in the whole score, urged Trojan to create a kind of double architecture. The orchestra has its own thematic material that flows coherently from act to act; however, each act bends the themes and the musical grammar to a strong *sound characterization* of contexts and characters. That is to say, Trojan proceeded to variate the music in accordance with melodic, harmonic and timbrical *signals* that conventionally evoke certain places or people: for example, exotic harmonies for the African forest, a brass band for the American Navy, menacing percussions for India and its perils, a march for the Australian gold-diggers, and so on. The ariettas, recitative, and choruses have small, stand-alone closed forms, and are superimposed (but complementary) to the orchestral discourse.

The need for characterization is addressed by Trojan also by means of a further sound idea that would find its best incarnation in Trnka's cinema: the imitation of noises and non-musical events with the orchestra and its instruments. *Merry-Go-Round* features musical onomatopoeias that stand for the growl of a gorilla, or for the sounds a merry-go-round makes when operated; in Trnka's film, *The Emperor's Nightingale*, Trojan would successfully imitate a singing nightingale with the high notes of a solo violin. Trojan's ability in this would allow Trnka to choose a silent cinema aesthetic (with no other sounds except music) for the films he authored in the first part of his career as a director (see Chapter 4). It was not unprecedented, at the beginning of the 1940s, to find such onomatopoeic use of musical instruments in an opera; Giacomo Puccini, for example, imitated a barrel organ with three flutes in *Il tabarro* (1918), and also required the use of an actual boat siren; he did similar naturalistic experiments with the tolling bells in *Tosca* (1899). In the 1940s, sound films had already acquainted audiences and composers with soundtracks that included also recorded sound effects, so the idea of noises intermingled with underscoring music was becoming popular. However, Trojan's onomatopoeias are not intended to be inherently innovative; they instead reaffirm the evocative power of music. With accurate and knowledgeable writing, any timbre, or combination thereof, could influence the listener to hear something that it is not supposed to come from musical instruments, but from events in the everyday life. Trojan's choice in this serves as a powerful commentary on his – apparently – double-faced approach to musical aesthetics: on the one hand, Trojan would always prefer to write functional music at the service of another art or another creative personality; that is to say, music based on an "external stimulus"* (Vičar 1989: 51). On the other hand, his stage and film music would also easily make its way to stand-alone suites, to be performed in concert, without actors or film projections; as Vladimír Štěpánek and Bohumil Karásek put it, Trojan's music does not merely explain a story, but creates an independent counterpoint to it that joins the images and enhances their effectiveness (Štěpánek and Karásek 1964: 137). So Trojan's musical onomatopoeias express a similar duality: they are dependent on memories of external events extraneous to music in order to be appreciated; however, they are actually pure music that does not need any complement in order to achieve its evocative effect.

Another sound that prominently featured in *Merry-Go-Round* is that of children's voices. Even though the four main characters are played by adult performers, the opera calls for the presence of a children's choir: Trojan had in mind the ensemble of Jan Kühn, but the use he made of such vocal timbres was not just a matter of circumstance and chance. In fact, child voices (solos or choirs) are a recurrent presence in Trojan's music, and they are a typical part of the soundscape of Trnka's films, often with a strong narrative role. For example, in *Bajaja* the singing of children appears

---

* "Vnější podnět."

during the titles that articulate the episodes of the film, commenting on the developments of the story; adult singing voices have important roles (Bajaja himself; the magical horse), but they are diegetic sounds, that is to say: they express the actual voices of the characters (see chapter 4). The children's choir, instead, sings outside of the story, framing it and ideally addressing the spectator from a different point of view (extradiegetic). The same extradiegetic role is given to children also in *The Czech Year*.

Choruses have actually a longstanding tradition of extradiegetic (or quasi-extradiegetic) presences since the ancient Greek tragedies where the chorus was a collective character, commenting on the action. In *Merry-Go-Round*, Trojan reprised this use. Other composers did so before him, from the beginnings of opera; Claudio Monteverdi, for example, entrusted an emotional commentary of the main action to the chorus in his opera *L'Orfeo* (*Orpheus*), that premiered in 1607. The fact that Trojan gives such a role to child singers, however, tacitly subverts the supposed authoritativeness of the choral mass. The extradiegetic choir, when not supposed to represent a collectivity participating in the action (thus prone to fault, like the village women in Act II, Scene 4 of Gaetano Donizetti's *L'elisir d'amore*), represents a wise voice in an opera; it advances interpretations, conclusions, and teachings about the tribulations of the protagonists on stage. Giving such a role to children seems to reinforce the fact that the opera is written with a young audience in mind: the spectator is implicitly invited to accept that it is children who have final word on the meaning of the story, as the *authority* that comments on the story sings with the voices of little ones. This trait of *Merry-Go-Round* also strongly affirms the value that the child perspective had in Trojan's poetics as a whole, as a key to a direct, relatable, and constraint-free way of emotive expression: Vičar even called Trojan, as an artist, a "sensitive *big child*"* (1989: 68).

---

* "Citlivým *velkým dítětem*."

The last major stylistic element that *Merry-Go-Round* features, and that remains as a constant in the later works of the mature Trojan and in Trnka's films, is folklore. Trojan's opera does not quote actual Czech songs or melodies, like would have happened in other compositions that focused on the reinterpretation of such repertoire, like *Zlatá brána* (*The Golden Gate*, 1973), which was incidental music based on Bohemian, Moravian, and Slovakian folk motifs. *Merry-Go-Round* uses folklore only as a model in order to achieve a special clarity through the use of simple formal structures and melodic profiles, potentially familiar to a wide audience. This simplicity counterbalances the timbrical and harmonic research, making it more understandable and less demanding in terms of relatability.

It might be argued, however, that the term *folklore* is wrongly applied to *Merry-Go-Round* because this opera has no direct links with historical popular songs and the like. This observation actually leads to a wider problem in Czech musicology, which is the definition of Czech folk music. The repertoire covered by this term is wide and complex: the expression identifies "the mythical creativity of subservient sections of rural population before the period of industrialization, but not as a whole. This term covers only a certain part of their musical activity, namely secular folk songs employing Czech texts and instrumental music" (Pilková 1988: 158). Czech folk music is not even homogeneous: "while this term is still commonly used by musicologists, ethnographers prefer the terms *folk music of Bohemia* and *folk music of Moravia*" (Pilková 1988: 161). This set of problems suggests that the so-called *folklore* of certain Czech compositions, which seems to pay homage to a traditional repertoire, is sometimes a matter of "accidental melodic or metro-rhythmic coincidence, which can be thoroughly misleading" (Pilková 1988: 163). Nonetheless, Vičar used the term *folklore* to speak of *Merry-Go-Round*. This *folklore*, though, is not a precise reference to a certain set of songs or dances, as already specified; nor is it an accidental use of musical features that revive memories from that tradition. Instead, it might be more correctly identified as a *folk-like* attitude of the composer, who borrows from the past of popular music a feeling of spontaneous musical creativity in accordance with his own communicative concerns, as well as with a free-flowing narration of childhood fantasy adventures. *Merry-Go-Round*'s spontaneity is actually a precise artistic goal of the work, superimposed to an elaborate set of modernist musical features. This contrast imbues the opera with a peculiar inner tension that propels the action in a compelling way: the "folk-like" spontaneity entices the ear, while the timbrical and harmonic research challenges the mind.

Trojan would often return to such tension in his scores for Trnka, expanding the boundaries of his personal approach to the idea of folklore, again with the use of formal unity in thematic diversity and fragmentation, surprising musical onomatopoeias, singing voices of children, and a folk-like attitude to complement the complex neoclassical approach to composition and dramatic narration.

CHAPTER 4

The Films by Trnka and Trojan

Jiří Trnka's career as a director lasted 20 years, from his debut hand-drawn short film *Grandpa Planted a Beet* (1945) to his sour farewell to puppet animation, *The Hand* (1965). In both cases, Vacláv Trojan was at the director's side, providing music for his animated images. In between, Trnka authored 23 more short films and five full-length features; Trojan scored 15 of those shorts (including the aforementioned first and last) and all five of his colleague's features. In the first ten years of Trnka's directorial activity, Trojan worked with him on at least one film per year: this rhythm was interrupted only by Trnka's hiatus of 1957–1959, when he dedicated himself to illustration. After the works of 1958–1959 (the short *Proč UNESCO* [*Why UNESCO?*], 1958, and the feature *A Midsummer Night's Dream*, 1959), Trnka greatly reduced his production; he directed just three more shorts before his retirement. Trojan returned only for the concluding *The Hand*.

Trojan's music marked the majority of the efforts by Trnka as an author of short films, and the totality of his results in full-length feature making. The preference that Trnka accorded to Trojan was evident; their cooperation was not devoid of conflicts and problems, though, because of their contrasting personalities (see Chapter 2). However, their films do not exude anything of such difficulties, as their artistic affinity covered up for all the divergences, providing to the history of animation one of the most conspicuous and coherent repertoires of a composer-director couple.

ZASADIL DĚDEK ŘEPU (GRANDPA PLANTED A BEET, 1945)

The first film Trnka ever directed was a hand-drawn short feature. According to Boček (1965: 75) Trnka wrote it to be a puppet piece even before he was contacted by the artists of the future Bratři v triku studio; however, he later decided to tell his story with animated drawings designed by himself.

The almost ten-minute short tells about an old farmer who plants a beet seed into the ground: he personally defends it from birds, parasites, and adverse weather conditions, to the point that he even *directs* the sun to shine or set with his hands. At night, his wife and daughter have dinner with him, together with their pets, a dog, and a cat. A mouse inhabits their house, too. While asleep, the farmer dreams about the beet and the parasites attacking it; so he wakes up and goes outside to check his precious vegetable. He finds it in the process of becoming uncannily gigantic; the next morning, the beet keeps growing, so the farmer decides to pull it out from the ground. However, his sole strength is not enough; so his family joins him in the effort. Only when also the tiniest member of the family, the mouse, comes to help, is the beet retrieved: but it runs over the whole group, making them roll away with it, as it starts to swirl and dance in the air. Stuck in the leaves of the beet, the farmer and his family look at the audience and have a hearty laugh.

For the first time, Trnka's drawings express their dramatic potential with movement; their appearance is faithful to the style the artist had used until that point in his illustrated books; it is, at the same time, quite distant from the leading style that was considered referential in hand-drawn animation at the time, that is to say, the Disney model. Trnka did not even adhere to the other American models (Felix the Cat by Otto Messmer and Pat Sullivan, or the Fleischer brothers) that were popular with pioneers of Czech animation, like the Dodals (see Chapter 1); instead, he used an original graphic design that emphasized the two-dimensional nature of the images, even though the visuals consistently suggested that the characters and their space were three-dimensional (as seen in the scene where the beet tumbles through the air). This choice is a departure from the solid design typical of U.S. animation in the 1940s. Such contrast between flatness and depth is also brought forward by the freely contradictory use of perspective, together with flat graphic patterns applied to items which are thick in volume, like the bedsheets, and the use of pure color gradients or textures instead of drawn details in the background. The acting and movement style is fluid but simple; sometimes the pacing is slowed down, especially when the editing refrains from using cuts to synthesize the events (but Trnka accentuates some moments by using zoom-ins); for example, when Grandpa mistakenly buries an earthworm, instead of the beet seed, some secondary actions take a few seconds of screen time, like when the character blows his nose; this creates the illusion of a long take and renders the visual narration less goal-oriented. The expressiveness of the faces is not overstressed. Just like in Trnka's future puppet films, the eyes of the characters are important catalysts of emotions, but they do not univocally suggest a single emotional state. What they evoke is an emotional range: this pensive vagueness is achieved with a design that lets the gaze point towards a slightly undefined direction. The eyes are in fact almond-shaped, and the irises are circular and big, so, they do not have a lot of space to move around. Thus, the gaze directions are limited by the design, and the big irises seem to look into the distance. The constraint on the gaze is reinforced by the presence of a half-closed upper eyelid that further reduces the area around the iris while giving the face a slightly sad expression.

The music by Trojan follows Trnka's stylistic lead: it reimagines and supersedes the clichés of cartoon music. The main strategy by which it interacts with the animation is a soft Mickey-Mousing, that is to say, the translation of every narrative movement on screen into musical trajectories (Chion 2001: 53). It is a strategy that was consolidated in the early Mickey Mouse cartoons; hence its name. However, it is a *soft* occurrence of it, because the translation of movements into sounds is not continuous; moreover, the strategy is not applied with the narrative efficiency of American cartoons, where the Mickey-Mousing punctuates the visual events necessary to the narrative goal of a sequence, or to define the development and payoff of a gag. In *Grandpa Plants a Beet*, Trojan creates irregular synchronization patterns, that sometimes underscore secondary events, like the sudden barking of a dog at the table where Grandpa is having his soup (mimicked by a trumpet), and sometimes ignores them, as in the aforementioned moment when the character blows his nose. Moreover, Trojan's Mickey-Mousing is strongly onomatopoeic: it is not only a matter of movement made into musical trajectories, but a quite precise imitation of the expected sound produced by the event on screen (see Chapter 3). Musical trajectories still happen, as when a crow pulls the earthworm off the ground, and the woodwind imitates the tugs of the animal's head and the stretching of the bug, with a contrast between high-pitched ascending scale fragments and lower, descending ones. However, the moments when a violin imitates a cat, or a piccolo suggests the squeaking of a mouse, present a more distinguished inventiveness. *Grandpa Plants a Beet* does not relinquish traditional sound effects altogether (there are a few, like the cawing of the crow), but makes a bold step forward in the use of a purely musical soundtrack; so, it can be considered a general rehearsal of the audiovisual aesthetic that Trnka and Trojan would used in feature-length films.

The slow-paced long takes by Trnka are accompanied by melodic episodes based on simple, folk-like tunes, in accordance with the rural setting of the story. For example, the arrival of the woman and the child presents the main theme of the short, based on the initial half of an ascending major scale. Nursery rhymes and children's songs in general often make use of such scale fragments; in fact, the melodic profile of Trojan's theme (C_3-D_3-E_3-F_3-G_3-G_3-A_3-A_3-G_3-A_3-A_3-G_3-G_3-F_3-F_3-E_3) is not far from that of *Ah! vous dirai-je, maman* (*Twinkle, Twinkle, Little Star*: C_3-C_3-G_3-G_3-A_3-A_3-G_3-F_3-F_3-E_3-E_3-D_3-D_3-C_3), the 18th-century French popular song that inspired Wolfgang Amadeus Mozart's piano *Variations KV 265*. The possible Mozart reference makes sense in light of Trojan's interest in neoclassicism (see Chapter 3).

ZVÍŘÁTKA A PETROVŠTÍ (THE ANIMALS AND THE BANDITS, 1946)

Trnka and Trojan's second collaboration was again a hand-drawn short: Trnka directed three films of this sort in 1946 (see Filmography). Meanwhile, in the same year, Trojan practiced music for animation with another director at a different studio, the state-owned Československý státní film, by writing for *Vodník ve mlýně* (*The Vodník in the Mill*, Josef Vácha, 1946): it was another hand-drawn production, that again allowed for an onomatopoeic use of the music, instead of sound effects. The character design was a bit closer to the Disney model, because of a certain attention to solid drawing and the use of the *slice-of-pie* light reflection in the irises of the characters, just like in the early Mickey Mouse design; however, the story was distinctively bohemian, as it featured the Vodník, a mythical aquatic creature that has been part of Czech folklore since the 14th century (Máchal 1995: 140).

The story of *The Animals and the Bandits* came from the Grimm brothers' tale *The Town Musicians of Bremen*: although the film focuses solely on the night episode of the animals scaring away the bandits from their hideout. There is a goat in place of the dog and the donkey from the original tale.

The short introduced a few novelties in the language of Trnka. The most remarkable was the dramatic use of camera movements: the zoom-ins that accentuated some key actions in *Grandpa Plants a Beet* were now accompanied by an improved inventiveness in taking advantage of peculiar points of view and editing solutions that only animation could allow. The most remarkable case is the visual idea that closes the film: a leaf with a hole detaches from a tree and is carried by the wind. As the camera follows the floating leaf, the hole lines up with the spectator's point of view and periodically works as an iris to focus on the characters in the background; it leaves them and then returns, to show how their action evolved. The hole in the leaf creates the editing in the sequence, that would have otherwise been a regular long take (Figure 4.1).

The Animals and the Bandits is also the first work by Trnka featuring a voice-over by a narrator. This element is not a common occurrence in the first half of the director's film career; it is however something Trnka needed to come to terms with, sometimes, to make the storytelling more effective. Meaningfully, the narrator of *The Animals and the Bandits* is a child; the vocal timbre of children would become a stylistic constant in films by Trnka and Trojan, as a signal of sincere closeness to their target audience.

Finally, *The Animals and the Bandits* contains some visual homages to Disney, that are in partial contrast with the stylistic

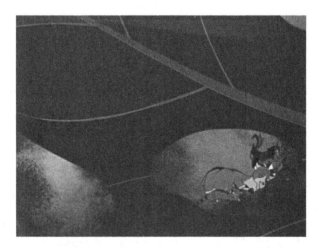

FIGURE 4.1 The hole in the leaf, used as an iris, at the end of *Zvířátka a Petrovští* (*The Animals and the Bandits*, 1946). (From Národní filmový archiv/National Film Archive [NFA], Prague. With permission.)

distancing from the United States seen in *Grandpa Plants a Beet*. However, such homages are circumstantiated and do not influence the rest of the design, which actually confirms the expressive solutions used by Trnka in his previous short. The referenced work is *Fantasia* (James Algar et al., 1940), and especially the *Nutcracker* episode: from its visual repertoire come the ideas of the leaf floating in the air and of the dancing mushroom, that emulate the ones animated by Art Babbitt for Disney, down to the little drops of dew adorning their caps. The camera movements that travel through the trees and leaves might be yet another *Fantasia* reference, as they remind one of the illusions of depth and focus given by the multiplane camera, a device in use at Disney studios since 1937, that allowed parallax effects by shooting frame by frame through a series of distanced, sliding, and transparent image layers.

The *Fantasia* references could be a consequence of the music-image relationship chosen for this film: as in the Disney feature, *The Animals and the Bandits* uses a pre-existing composition from the *classical** repertoire and sets the animation to it. However, the presence of the narrator's voice partly contradicts the model.

Trnka entrusted Trojan with the adaptation of music from Act 5 of the 1908 ballet *From Fairy Tale to Fairy Tale*, by Czech composer Oskar Nedbal: that part of the original work dealt with the tale of *The Town Musicians of Bremen*. Trojan intervened on the junction and cuts between the ballet numbers in order to smoothen the change of atmospheres and the connections between of otherwise separated pieces of music. The audiovisual style does not use a synchronization with a grade of sound-image correspondence similar to that of *Fantasia*, though: there is much more freedom, and some animation that could have offered an excuse for musical events, in a Disney context, pass here unnoticed by the soundtrack: an example is the fearful jolt the animals suddenly make in the forest. There are synchronizations, anyway,

---

* The term *classical* is not here referring to the actual classical period in music (1750–1820), but to its common and popular use: art music that does not leave much space to improvisation.

but they are not overtly evident, because the animation does not overstress them: for example, the steps of the bandits in the forest are synchronized with the rhythm of the music. In general, though, it is the musical mood that is illustrated by Trnka, and not the minute details of the score.

If *Fantasia* was really a model for *The Animals and the Bandits*, the main inspiration that Trnka took from it was then the chance to completely forfeit recorded dialogue and sound effects, in favor of a purely musical soundtrack in charge of every acoustic feature of the film.

ŠPALIČEK (THE CZECH YEAR, 1947)

After *The Animals and the Bandits*, Trnka further explored the possibilities of the animated cartoon, by using different themes and alternative designs, and entering the territories of artistic (*Dárek, The Gift*, 1946; music by Jan Rychlík) and political satire (*Pérák a SS, The Springer and the SS*, 1946; music by Jan Rychlík); in 1947, he co-directed with Stanislav Látal *Liška a džbán* (*The Fox and the Jug*; music by Jan Kapr). However, when he decided to leave drawings for puppet animation, the result of his efforts bore certain similarities to *The Animals and the Bandits*. There are two remarkable affinities between the 1946–1947 short and Trnka's first full-length feature, *The Czech Year*: they were both structured around the idea of fairy tales as seen from the Czech perspective, and their atmospheres and communicative strategies were strongly determined by a musical score. As noted above, *The Animals and the Bandits* was based on a fragment of a ballet titled *From Fairy Tale to Fairy Tale*. *The Czech Year* is not a collection of universally known fairy tales, but a sequence of six episodes that present customs, holidays, and celebrations relevant to the Czech tradition; sometimes they have a story, sometimes they just present a situation and its variations. However, the original title of *The Czech Year, Špaliček*, actually has a specific meaning: it indicates an anthology of folk tales, poems, and songs, that is to say, a miscellaneous treasury, intended to preserve the disappearing cultural heritage of the Czech country. The term *špaliček* was popularized by two early 20th century printed collections by Mikoláš Aleš (see Chapter 2). So, *The Czech Year* was actually a collection of folk tales, just like Nedbal's ballet; the connection with the originating source of *The Animals and the Bandits* is even reinforced by the possibility that Trnka took some structural inspiration for his feature from another ballet, *Špaliček* by Martinů.

As for the importance of music to *The Czech Year*, it would be wrong to say that the animation is an attempt at visualizing the score, like in Disney's *Fantasia*. The film actually relies upon a pre-existing musical repertoire, constituted by folk songs: they come from collections compiled by Karel Jaromír Erben, František Bartoš, Čeněk Holas, Jindřich Jindřich, and Jaromír Horáček (Vičar 1989: 111). They are however rearranged and inserted by Trojan into a musical architecture with an attitude similar to that of the opera *Merry-Go-Round* (see Chapter 3): the original melody rests over a compellingly modernist harmonization and orchestration. It is not, thus, an attempt at simulating an *authentic* restitution of the folk repertoire; the songs are in fact modified in order to fit the narrative needs of the animation. The relationship between the visual and musical sides is reciprocal and integrated, to the point that Trojan is credited also as a story advisor in the opening titles: a detail that reveals the existence of artistic cross-exchanges of competences between the director and the composer.

The use of puppets influenced the musical choices, too. Trnka abandoned hand-drawn shorts out of doubt about the style required by their medium; he felt that it was inclined to "excessive grotesqueness, stylization, and hyperactivity" (Janeček in Česálková 2017: 123). The project of creating a puppet animation was developed by Trnka at the new studio (Loutkový film Praha) he set up with some trusted Bratři v triku artists, like Břetislav Pojar, who was to animate the piper in *The Czech Year* (Benešova 2009: 4), and Stanislav Látal. At first, his idea was to animate just a short film, based on his oil painting *Bethlehem* (see Chapter 2).

The film was then expanded into a full-length feature, with the addition of five more shorts: *Masopust (Carnival)*, *Jaro (Spring)*, *Legenda o sv. Prokopu (Legend of St. Prokop)*, *Pouť (Pilgrimage)*, and *Posvícení (Festival)*. *Bethlehem* became the concluding segment.

Trnka borrowed from the puppet theater an acting aesthetic based on characters with unchangeable facial expressions (see the Introduction). The emotional focus of the animated performance was thus redistributed from the faces to other features: body language, film language (editing, framing, camera movements), and music.

Trnka alerts the spectator about the relevance of music in the feature by making the opening titles appear over images of a handwritten score; the title card of the film is a close-up of the title at the beginning of the musical manuscript. As soon as the film starts, however, it feels and looks as though the images determine the music: the puppets are given singing voices and they play musical instruments, so the music seems to originate from the scene, and not vice versa. There is no lip synching, of course; however, the dance moves of the puppets, strongly reinforced by compelling camerawork and editing that create an energic rhythmic pulse, with swift shifts between characters and details, create a convincing diegetic impression: the protagonists seem to be playing and singing beyond the screen. The diegetic illusion is strengthened by the use of children's voices. The problem of the vocal timbre to use in puppet performances had always been a relevant concern in this field: Skupa, for example, cared to develop a distinct style of voice acting for his theatrical shows (see Chapter 1). It was Trojan who suggested the used of children's voices instead of counterfeited adult voices, after his previous experiences with *Merry-Go-Round* and Kühn's children's choir; that ensemble also performs in *The Czech Year*, along with the Filmový symfonický orchestra (Film Symphony Orchestra) conducted by Otakar Pařík (who interpreted almost all the scores Trojan wrote for Trnka). In Trojan's opinion, the visual appearance of puppets suggested that they should have voices similar to those of children (Vičar 1989: 111); this choice remained in most of the following films by Trnka and Trojan, with a few rare exceptions of puppets singing with the voice of an adult, like in *Prince Bajaja*. The first episode of *The Czech Year, Carnival*, might be a manifesto to this vocal poetics, new to Czech puppetry: the animation and the cinematography repeatedly affirm that what the audience hears comes from those puppets, by consistently showing characters content to play their instruments and to make gestures that reinforce the content of the lyrics sung by children voices. This sets the music as diegetic, that is to say coming from the diegesis, or the world of the story, beyond the screen: the spectator believes themselves to be listening to the same sounds that the characters on screen are supposed to be hearing.

Only in the second episode, *Spring*, the preoccupation with creating a perceivable association between puppet acting and music becomes less urgent: the moments when the characters are shown in non-musical situations, like climbing a tree, are more frequent. The visual presence of musical instruments is anyway a constant throughout the whole of *The Czech Year*; as the film progresses, though, Trojan is less concerned with making realistic sound-image associations. The instruments on screen are often not the ones actually providing the sound, even though there are naturalistic touches, like calculated dissonances that create the impression of amateurish, improvised music by simple people, and the composer associates musical sounds with objects played by children, like funnels and pots.

It is like the authors, after having sufficiently informed the audience about the diegetic value of the musical score, start to feel safe about it: the audiovisual association becomes thus more imaginative. The final point of this process is reached when the music starts to imitate the singing of birds; later, in the same episode, it simulates the thunderous sound of a storm. This is not just dramatic underscoring, adhering to the international film music tradition centered in Hollywood, and inspired by the 19th-century repertoire of program music (as in Ludwig Van Beethoven's

"Pastoral" Symphony, Hector Berlioz's Symphonie Fantastique, or Franz Liszt's symphonic poems). That is to say, the music here does not just repeat the narrative content, by interpreting the feelings connected with the thunderstorm: it becomes the sound of the thunderstorm itself, instead. Without music, the scene would be completely silent, with no sound effects. It is by subtracting the conventional sound synchronies of the sound film that Trojan and Trnka maximize the diegetic potential of the music: basically, they abandon the traditional diegetic illusion and let the music freely dispose of the void left by it. It is not the first time that such aesthetics appeared in the history of cinema; it was previously used in several silent films that did not have any simulated sound diegesis by default. In those films, the audience was not expecting sound synchronies; when they happened, the music might momentarily shift from the extradiegetic to the diegetic level, becoming an acoustic consequence of some visual cause. This audiovisual function is specific to silent films, or to films that are not expected to provide a synchronic simulation of a sound diegesis. It might be called an *interdiegetic* function (Bellano 2013: 66).

In order for this audiovisual freedom of association to be effective, Trojan and Trnka had to be sure about what the audience was expecting from their film. This is why the beginning of *The Czech Year* overstressed the diegetic value of the music. This preoccupation with the statement of clear audiovisual expectations would return also in the openings of other films by the same authors. The music of *The Czech Year* reaches its least diegetic value halfway through the picture, during the episode of the *Legend of St. Prokop*; there, it becomes more of an emotional underscoring, or comment, to the mimic action (there is no narrating voice), with occasional Mickey-Mousing ideas, like when an ascending flute scale describes the stringing of a bow.

However, as the conclusion of the film approaches, the diegetic approach resurfaces; *Bethlehem* is again about a crowd of characters playing and singing. The circular connection with the audiovisual setting of *Carnival*, the opening segment, is even confirmed by a small detail: among the instruments shown in *Bethlehem*, there is a dulcimer (cimbál, in Czech) (Figure 4.2). In *Carnival* this instrument is absent, but the lyrics of the very first folk song say, "How on earth shall we buy a dulcimer?"

The ubiquitous nature of the diegesis in *The Czech Year* is important to the point it becomes a story element in the *Festival* segment, when the animated puppets attend a show of stringed puppets. The situation poses a clever visual paradox that invites a momentary break of the diegetic illusion; when puppets are shown looking at other puppets, the spectator is implicitly reminded of the true nature of the film *actors*: they are animated objects. There is, anyway, a visual signal that shows the difference between the puppets that stand for real people, and the stringed puppets: the latter have a rougher design. After a while, though, the stringed puppets come alive as actor-puppets in the imagination of a character; so, they are given the same detailed appearance as their audience. The diegesis reshapes its status quo, just like it does through the whole film, when freely attaching or disengaging from the

FIGURE 4.2 The dulcimer player in the concluding episode of *Špalíček* (*The Czech Year*, 1947). (From Národní filmový archiv/National Film Archive [NFA], Prague. With permission.)

music, in a continuous play with the audiovisual instincts of the spectator.

CÍSAŘŮV SLAVÍK (THE EMPEROR'S NIGHTINGALE, 1949)

The next project Trnka and Trojan undertook was a new full-length feature, but not divided into short segments this time. It told a story from a famous fairytale, *Nattergalen* (*The Nightingale*) by Hans Christian Andersen. The basic narrative arc remained the same as the original source: a Chinese emperor is deeply touched by the singing of a nightingale, so he commands that the bird be caught and brought to his court. One day, he is gifted with a mechanical nightingale; he then loses interest in the real bird, which leaves. The emperor pays attention only to the clattering sounds of the ingenious machine, until the artificial bird eventually breaks down, and the emperor fells severely ill; the nightingale then returns and, with its moving singing, convinces Death to spare the life of his former master.

The main plot point of Andersen's tale, the illusory beauty of a puppet bird, was particularly fit to be developed into a puppet feature; the resulting visuals, moreover, would have reprised the ironic contrast between the different statuses of the puppets on screen, like in the puppet play sequence from *The Czech Year*: in the diegetic reality beyond the screen, most puppets would have been situated as *real* people or animals; the mechanical bird, instead, was to be qualified as artificial for both the spectators and the other actor-puppets.

The music by Trojan further developed this diegetic interplay about reality and its imitation: the film embraces again a silent film aesthetic, with the music working as a substitute for almost the whole soundtrack with very sporadic concessions to sound effects. There is a significant exception to this choice: the beginning and end of the puppet film are framed by live-action sequences, featuring a boy and a girl; the condition of the boy mirrored that of the puppet emperor (that Trnka designs as a child), pampered with every possible extravagant gift, but very lonely nonetheless. The animated portion of *The Emperor's Nightingale* is then set as a dream of the feverish boy about his toys. The live-action part is without dialogue too, but there are much more sound effects. The English-dubbed version presents a voice-over narration by Boris Karloff, written by Phyllis McGinley; there was no spoken narration in the Czech original. There is one striking difference from *The Czech Year*: just like in *Grandpa Plants a Beet*, the musical score does not feature voices that sing lyrics at all. It is a purely instrumental work, with occasional interventions of vocalizations from a children's chorus.

The Emperor's Nightingale was not the first animated or musical transposition of Andersen's tale: in 1927, Lotte Reiniger directed a silhouette short film titled *Die chinesische Nachtigall*. Igor Stravinsky composed a three-act short opera, titled *Le rossignol* (1914, rev. 1962); part of it later became a 1917 tone poem (*The Song of the Nightingale*), used also as ballet music by a Sergej Diaghilev production in 1920.

There is only one point in common, between Stravinsky's version and Trojan's score: the choice to simulate the voice of the nightingale with a musical instrument. Stravinsky briefly used the violin to do so, but he mostly chose the flute; after all, the sound emission of most living creatures is based on principles similar to those of wind instruments, which set a column of air into vibration. Trojan, instead, made a more daring move by always assigning the role of the bird to a solo violin. The instrument is in fact capable of a sound that imitates that of a wind instrument, with a technique known as flageolet, which uses light touches of the fingers on the strings, while bowing with care, to produce high-pitched harmonics. Trojan could count on a performer who mastered this technique, Ivan Kawaciuk, a member of the Film Symphony Orchestra; it was precisely because of this musician's ability that he confidently gave to the violin the role of the bird, after having considered using the voice of a boy from Kühn's choir. However, the boy he had in mind went through puberty and voice change; so, Trojan had to modify his plans (Vičar 1989: 115–117). In the score, a similar onomatopoeic attitude is present in the piece called *Žabák* (*The Frog*), that uses a trombone *wah-wah* effect to *dub* the singing voice of a frog.

The violin solo that *voices* the nightingale is not just an onomato-poeic imitation of the call of the bird, even though it is interwoven with tremolos that distinctly recall what a real nightingale might sing. It works instead as a melodic theme, with a distinct charac-ter and profile: Trojan makes it one of the *leitmotifs*, or conducting themes, of the score. The use of leitmotifs is a typical feature of many film scores; it was a simplified version of the leitmotif architecture found in Richard Wagner's operas (hence the German term that identifies this audiovisual strategy). It was exported to American classic cinema and widely used by Austrian or German composers who had emigrated to the United States in the 1920s and 1930s, like Max Steiner, Erich Wolfgang Korngold, and Franz Waxman. A leitmotif-based film score uses recognizable melodies (or frag-ments thereof) in association with recurring protagonists, things, places, or emotions, in order to signal the relevance they have in a certain moment of a film. Each leitmotif gets varied and rearranged according to the dramatic needs of the scenes they are featured in.

Resorting to the leitmotif function was probably, for Trojan, a means to deal with a full-length film score with a single narrative arc: the return of recognizable themes unifies the musical archi-tecture. It was not, thus, a passive concession to the "*Hollywood*" style of film music writing, but a strategic move to transition from the short format of *The Czech Year* to the time span of a unitary feature film. Arthur Hepner (1951: 7) identified four leitmotifs:

> "A haunting lament to represent the sadness of the kitchen maid, [...] a monotonous song of the mechanical bird [...] [,] a motif of tension, a squared-off phrase, to convey the binding regime and routine that always surrounds the Emperor [...][,] and finally the song of the real nightin-gale. [...] Besides the principal motifs there are numerous subsidiary ones, each relating to one of the multitude of subordinate details in the film story."

Hepner does not elaborate on the "squared-off phrase," that debuts in the live-action segment of *The Emperor's Nightingale* as a piano exercise played by the boy, guided by the inexorable clicking of a metronome. Vičar reported twice (1989: 115; 2005: 44) that Trojan took that theme from the didactical compositions by Ferdinand Beyer (curiously calling him *Bayer* on both occasions), the author of one of the piano methods for beginners most widely in use. However, in the *Vorschule im Klavierspiel Op. 101* (1851) there is no trace of such a theme; instead, the melodic contour and the rhythm of the first phrase in Trojan's piece are literally identical to those of the beginning of the aria *Vedrai, carino* from Mozart's *Don Giovanni KV 527*. It might be that Trojan used a simple, famous, and captivating theme to create an exercise *à la Beyer*; in fact, even though no piece from Beyer's *Op. 101* gets explicitly quoted, Trojan uses the same elementary phrasing and harmonic rhythm that appear in several exercises from the *Vorschule im Klavierspiel*, like in nos. 18 and 19; furthermore, the melodic contour of no. 9 is distantly similar to that of *Vedrai, carino*, and subsequently to that of Trojan's composition. Anyway, the dramatic meaning of the music is clear: through the use of Beyer-like phrasing and harmony, as well as of two-voice writing that imitates that of many piano exercises for beginners, Trojan seeks a parallel between the tedious, entrapping routine of young musicians and the court obligations of the child emperor.

Hepner talked also of a "Chinese flavor" of the music, but Trojan concedes almost nothing to the stereotyped conventions that signify *Chinese music* to the ear of the average Western listener. On the contrary, *The Emperor's Nightingale* furthers the merge between a modernist language (Hepner compares it to that of Hindemith, Bartók, and the early Schönberg; 1951: 8) and Czech folk tunes. The score even quotes the popular song *Jede, jede poštovský panáček* (*Here Comes the Postman*), in the scene where the mail coach delivers the mechanical nightingale to the emperor. For the rest, a kind of exotic flavor is conveyed by the use of unusual instruments, like "rattles, tapers, small bells, electric saws, Chinese nuts, a xylophone, and other percussion instruments" (Vičar 2005: 44). The only moment when a cliché in Chinese musical writing is in use is in the song of the mechanical nightingale. The obsessive refrain, that almost pierces the ear by using high-pitched sounds from plucked strings, is built on a pentatonic scale. Western audiences learnt to match Oriental suggestions with pentatonic (*five-sound*) scales from at least as early as the exotic musical vogue of late 19th–early 20th century, thanks to authors like Claude Debussy; even Stravinsky widely used pentatonic scales in his *Le rossignol*. Trojan specifically uses one of the five basic Chinese pentatonic scales, the shāng (商). By confining it solely to the singing of the fake bird, however, he implicitly makes a connection between the false beauty of the mechanical contraption and the empty use of musical stereotypes in cinema; they want the spectator to believe they directly come from far-away people and lands, while actually being superficial fabrications. As an artist consciously engaged in the preservation and understanding of authentic folklore, Trojan might have seen in the dialectic between true and fake beauty, at the core of *The Emperor's Nightingale*, a commentary on the misunderstandings and prejudices connected with the popular use of the term *folk music* in contemporary culture.

ČERTŮV MLÝN (*THE DEVIL'S MILL*, 1949)

After his first two full-length features, Trnka embarked on the production of three short puppet films. All of them had a story that was strongly related to music; however, Trojan composed a score for only two of them: *Čertův mlýn* (*The Devil's Mill*, 1949) and *Román s basou* (*The Story of the Contrabass*, 1949). The third one, *Árie prérie* (*The Song of the Prairie*, 1949) was a small musical, with songs *interpreted* by puppets that, contrary to Trnka's usual standards, were given the ability to open their mouths and close their eyes in sync with the music. The idea of a parodistic musical in a Western film setting came from Jiří Brdečka, who also co-wrote *The Emperor's Nightingale*; he later reprised the idea in the live-action feature *Limonádový Joe aneb Koňská opera* (*Lemonade Joe, or the Horse Opera*, Oldřich Lipský, 1964), based on a novel and stage play of his. The music was by Jan Rychlík, just like in the 1964 film, who was a specialist in jazz music and a prominent contributor to the post-war Czech musical scene. The "American" and parodistic tone of *The Song of the Prairie* was maybe quite far from Trojan's *folk* sensibility, rooted in the Czech tradition; on top of that, *The Song of the Prairie* did not feature music as a key plot element. Its songs were musical numbers not integrated into the story: they were attractions, intended as surreal and unexpected substitutes for dialogues. Trojan's collaborations with Trnka, instead, dwelt on the composer's peculiar ability to interweave his scores with narratives based on relevant and diegetic musical elements: among them are the performers in *The Czech Year* and the bird in *The Emperor's Nightingale*. Consistently with this, *The Story of the Contrabass* is based on an incident involving the instrument mentioned in the title; *The Devil's Mill*, instead, tells about an itinerant old veteran who plays a broken barrel organ. At first, it produces very unpleasant music that drives away animals and people alike. When the veteran receives a new crank from a white-bearded man, the instrument starts to produce a melodious and uplifting melody. At night, the protagonist takes shelter in an abandoned watermill; as he sleeps, the devil arrives and starts to play pranks on him. However, the old man gets the better of him by playing the organ: the devil is caught in a rapturous dance. The next morning, the veteran, with a child, opens a dam and lets the wheel of the mill spin again, just like the crank of his organ.

Trnka recovers a character from *The Czech Year* – the barrel organ player – as well as the puppet design and acting aesthetics. There is however a major difference from his previous puppet features: the sound effects of *The Devil's Mill* are not substituted for and imitated by music. Noises, calls, creaks, and thumps are active parts of the soundtrack, in which the music disappears for relatively long stretches, in order to let the effects be heard and have a better dramatic impact. There are only a few instances of Trojan's onomatopoeic ideas, as when he renders the squeaking of bats with violins, or when he orchestrates the annoying dissonances of the broken barrel organ. For the rest, *The Devil's Mill* appears as an attempt to research a new sound aesthetic for puppet films, less abstractly lyrical and more concrete in its effects, which are nearly identical to real-life sounds. This might be another sign of Trnka's growing confidence in the suspension of disbelief that his puppet animation could induce in the audience, which seems to invite them to read the characters as stand-ins for real actors. Trnka never desired puppet films to compete with live-action cinema (and this is also why he decided to refrain from animating the faces of the characters); however, he wanted the audience to be taken in by the narration and to relate to the puppets as if they had thoughts and emotions. The sequence of the puppet theater in *The Czech Year*, with the presence of two kinds of puppets (the ones supposed to stand for *real people*, and the others presented as objects moved around by puppeteers) reveals how this aspect of Trnka's poetics is supposed to work; the numerous sound effects in *The Devil's Mill* confirm this attitude and further sends to the audience relatable impressions of life from the puppet world beyond the screen.

On the other hand, Trojan provided the film with musical atmospheres that work on a different level of emotional communication: the neoclassical roots of the composer's language revive memories from program music and tone poems of the past. When the protagonist wakes up in the morning after the battle with the devil, for example, the sunshine and bucolic air of the scene are commented on by a sort of paraphrase from the beginning of the fifth and last movement of Beethoven's *Pastoral Symphony*. The absence of dialogues lets music – when present – flow in ample lyrical arcs, without interruption.

ROMÁN S BASOU (THE STORY OF THE CONTRABASS, 1949)

The 1949 short *The Story of the Contrabass* set a series of firsts for Trnka. For the first time, his source was not Czech folklore or an original story, but literature: an 1886 short novel by Anton Pavlovič Čechov. It was also the first time a Trnka film had to deal with nudity, even though the story treatment, and the puppet design, managed to do so with a light, tasteful, and endearing touch. Finally, Trnka inserted sporadic and subtle animations into the eyes of the characters, to show fleeting moments of surprise (as when the protagonist emerges from the water and sees the lady asleep). However, the faces remained mostly adorned with fixed expressions. The short tells about a lady and a contrabass player who happen to take a swim in the same lake; after some thieves take away the woman's clothes, the musician offers the lady the chance to take shelter in his contrabass case. However, the case is later picked up by his fellow instrumentalists, who discover, to their astonishment, the naked woman inside.

Trojan's treatment of the contrabass as a leading instrument in his score is not pedantic at all. On the contrary, the sound of the solo instrument ironically shies away from taking center stage, as a witty counterpart to a tale about discretion and embarrassment of characters naked in spite of their will. At first, the contrabass is brashly presented as the soloist in a symphonic concert: the opening titles show a close-up on the strings and bow of a real instrument in an actual performance. As the puppet action starts, however, the music prefers a chamber writing with many concurrent soloists, that take turns in commenting on the scenes: the writing alternates the contrabass with a piano, a flute, and even a mandolin. After all, the place where the protagonist is supposed to perform is what seems to be a salon in a high-class mansion from the early 19th century: a small audience, dressed sumptuously, waits for a trio to play for them.

Trojan's concertante chamber score is less dependent on the screen action than in the previous films by Trnka, at least in respect to synchronies and onomatopoeias; there are, anyway, moments where the music suggests character voices (when the musicians call out for their colleague in the woods, horns are heard, mimicking their cries), and even a Mickey-Mousing for the impatient walk of a character waiting for the contrabass player in the mansion. The sound of a clock is the only effect that shares a place in the soundtrack with the music. The rest of *The Story of the Contrabass* is built as a silent film, and one with almost no need for diegetic suggestions: the music is free to proceed with relative freedom from the on-screen action, save for a constant emotional accordance with the events. This kind of musical *aloofness*, unusual for a Trnka–Trojan film, brings a further layer of humor to a tale based on the fragile and contradictory nature of human conventions: the dignified order of the concert hall is disrupted by the innocent nudity of a woman; a contrabass case might become a refuge and a sign of a man's gallantry, notwithstanding the fact that this gentleman is naked. Appearance is superficial, just like puppets are more then they appear in Trnka's animation.

BAJAJA (PRINCE BAJAJA, 1950)

Bajaja was the third feature film by Trnka and Trojan. It was inspired by a fairy tale written by Božena Němcová, a writer who is today considered one of the main contributors to the Czech National Revival of the 19th century. The tale was collected in her 1862 book *Národní báchorky a pověsti* (*National Stories and Legends*). It tells a story set in an imaginary Middle Age. Bajaja, a young villager living with his old father, is visited one night by a mysterious white horse. The animal is inhabited by the spirit of the young man's mother, who provides Bajaja with a magical sword, armor, and cloak: he is called to put his courage to the test, to save the soul of his mother in purgatory. He will slay three dragons with multiple heads, that menace the lives of three sister princesses. Later, during a feast for the liberation of the kingdom from the dragons, each one of the princesses is invited to drop an apple to the floor: they will marry the men who pick them up. The apple of the youngest and fairest princess is picked up by Bajaja; however, the girl does not recognize her savior and scorns him. The king organizes then a tournament, to find a groom for his daughter. Bajaja triumphs, disguised by his armor; however, he is now the one who rejects the princess. Only at night, he approaches the girl in her room and reveals to her his true identity, finally returning with her to his father's humble cottage.

Trnka recounts this tale by making pervasive use of pantomime, as was typical of all his puppet films until 1950. However, while in his previous features the pantomime was largely musical, meaning that there were almost no other sounds except music, *Bajaja* uses sound effects in synchrony with the actions, like applause and laughs. This choice became more common in Trnka's later films, where recorded dialogue also appeared, transitioning thus towards a sound film aesthetic. The presence of diegetic sound effects, though, seems to situate the film at the interface between silent and sound film. This allows the director and the musician to manage the diegesis and its sounds in a very flexible and expressively original way.

The narrative, visual, and musical style of *Bajaja* does not refer to specific myths of the Czech people. The tale by Němcová was used by Trnka and Trojan to create a vibrant sense of antiquity and tradition, without realistic historical references. As Vičar described: "This union of music and imagery established a remarkable synthesis, which included Gothic, Renaissance, and Romantic elements as well as court and folk themes [...]" (Vičar 2005: 45). It could be argued that the authors here celebrated the Czech National Revival by evoking the sole *feeling* of tradition associated with it, thus causing it to transcend into an aesthetic abstraction.

This abstractness might have helped the music achieve a peculiar universal and versatile quality that invited the composer to rework it many times in concert and stage versions. After the film, the music of Bajaja was reincarnated in a work for solo child voice, for children's choir and piano from 1950, a *Symphonic Suite* with a children's choir from 1951, a *Suite* for violin, guitar, and accordion from 1970, a *Suite* for flute, violin, viola, cello, and harp from 1971, a *Symphonic March* (*Princ Bajaja. Vítězný pochod*) from 1972, the *Nonetto Favoloso* from 1979, a *Suite* for accordion and electrophonic accordion from 1980, and the ballet *Prince Bajaja*, posthumously completed by Jan Klusák in 1986.

At the beginning of the film, a musical episode summarizes in a concise and consistent way the audiovisual aesthetics of *Bajaja*, by referring simultaneously to the thematic points mentioned above: the relationship between pantomime and diegetic illusion; the sense of tradition and antiquity; and the versatility of the musical ideas. At night, Bajaja witnesses the apparition of the white horse. The movements of the animal are rhythmically synchronized with the sound of strings playing pizzicato; whenever the horse stops, a singing voice is heard, uttering the three-syllable call *miláčku* (*my darling*), over a three-note descending motif (its first occurrence is F-E-B flat). Bajaja reacts both to the pizzicato strings and the call, meaning that he hears them. So, they are substitutes for diegetic sounds; however, they do not wake up Bajaja's father. It is thus heavily implied that those sounds are only heard by Bajaja's mind; this impression is reinforced by the intense montage that Trnka conjures up between Bajaja's face and the horse's eye, while the camera slowly zooms in and the speaking voice of the boy's mother is heard. The images tell about a connection between Bajaja and the animal (Figure 4.3): the final audiovisual staging is not diegetic, nor extradiegetic, but it might be interpreted as a *mediated* level, according to Sergio Miceli's terminology: the sound is shared between the inner mind of a character and the audience (Miceli 2009: 654–657). The use of very short motifs is typical of Trojan: Vičar noticed how, for example, his music is often built around an ascending four-note motif, made of the 6th, 8th, 9th, and 10th tones of the overtone series (for example: G-C-D-E, in

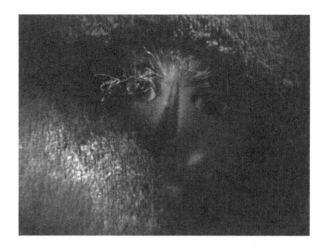

FIGURE 4.3   A crossfade between the eye of the mother-horse and the face of her son in *Bajaja* (*Prince Bajaja*, 1950). (From Národní filmový archiv/National Film Archive [NFA], Prague. With permission.)

C major; Vičar 2005: 43). The *miláčku* call in *Bajaja*, however, is different: it introduces a harmonic context that, to the ear, creates an impression of antiquity and folklore. It touches the 4th, 3rd, and 7th grades of a Phrygian dominant scale, one of the so-called Gypsy musical scales, associated with Indian, Middle Eastern, Eastern European, Central Asian, and Flamenco music.

Finally, when Bajaja leaves his father to follow his mother and face his destiny, the music transforms into a slow march. A musical phrase that responds to the main march theme features, again, the Phrygian dominant scale: its melody starts from the first two notes of the *miláčku* call, but then it substitutes the 7th with the 2nd grade (not B flat, but D flat). This march later became later a successful independent concert piece. In the *Nonetto Favoloso* of 1979, it appears briefly at the very end of the last movement, in a quiet rendition; this responds well to the atmosphere of this chamber piece, that takes from the original Bajaja mostly its nostalgic, fairy tale-like features (hence the Italian term *favoloso* in the title, which means *like a fairy tale*, but also *outlandish* or *strikingly beautiful*).

The diegetic freedom of Trnka and Trojan's audiovisual style is demonstrated also in the serenade sung by Bajaja to the princesses upon his arrival at the castle. The images by Trnka clearly show Bajaja playing a lute, with body language that closely follows the phrasing of the music: the spectator is thus invited to believe that the puppet is actually singing. However, Trojan does not use the sound of a real lute playing the music, but rather an electric piano. The diegesis, once again, is negated and creatively reinterpreted. The use of the Mixolydian mode, moreover, evokes here a feeling of ancient times, even though there is no folk connotation: the Mixolydian was the seventh of the eight church modes in use during the Middle Ages.

A remarkable occurrence of the way Trnka and Trojan intertwined their music and images is the gavotte that appears right after the serenade scene, while Bajaja is guided by the three princesses through the castle to meet the king. The gavotte was a European court dance that emerged in the late Renaissance, during the 16th century. This choice by Trojan is thus a further elaboration on the generic antiquity of the setting, in good resonance with the presence of a majestic castle in the scenography. The girls lead the boy with a playful attitude, often indulging in pirouettes; the graceful upper melody of the gavotte, played pizzicato by strings, catches their movements and the overall mood, reinforcing it. However, the bass line of the dance is unexpectedly thunderous and ominous. This unsettling aural presence finds a visual correspondence in the pitch-black spaces behind the spiral staircases that the characters sometimes climb, while lit in a sharply contrasting way (Figure 4.4). The final mood is contrasted as well; the reason behind this is revealed as the pantomime goes on, and Trnka alternates between the image of the grieving king, an hourglass, and a tapestry showing the three princesses and a falcon preying on a sheep. The ominous basses return in precise correspondence with the images of the hourglass and the tapestry: without any dialogue, Trnka and Trojan are describing the menace that impends on the princesses, who will soon be claimed by the fiery dragons. Those basses are, in a way, a substitute for the dragons, which the director and the

FIGURE 4.4   A frame from the spiral staircase scene in *Prince Bajaja*. (From Národní filmový archiv/National Film Archive [NFA], Prague. With permission.)

musician make much more terrifying by denying their revelation to the spectator until their confrontation with Bajaja. The individuality of such basses as a musical character is rendered particularly evident in Trojan's reworking of the gavotte in the 1970 *Suite* for violin, guitar, and accordion. The grave notes are given to the accordion alone, whose timbre, generated by a stream of air that puts reeds in vibration, is greatly different from that of the violin and guitar, which are stringed instruments. The accordion literally seems to be breathing as it is played: the association with a fire-breathing monster might not be completely accidental.

What Trnka and Trojan achieved in *Bajaja* is an expansion and generalization of their artistic research on Czech national traditions. Memories from the mythical past of their land were transformed into an aesthetic of nostalgia and antiquity, with a new universal appeal. While doing this, they also widened the scope of the audiovisual pantomime style of Czech puppet animation, by creating false diegetic sensations in the viewer, in a hybridization of the silent film style with that of the sound film.

VESELÝ CIRKUS (THE MERRY CIRCUS, 1951)

After *Prince Bajaja*, and before tackling a new full-length feature, Trnka momentarily set aside puppet animation. He worked on two short films based on a two-dimensional aesthetic, however very far from that of animated drawings. The first one, *Veselý Cirkus* (*The Merry Circus*, 1951) used stop-motion animation on paper cut-outs: flat puppets, made of modular, unchangeable parts, acted before pastel backgrounds; the art was by Trnka and three more illustrators, František Tichý, Kamil Lhoták, and Zdeňek Seydl. The other short, *O zlaté rybce* (*The Golden Fish*, 1951) was a montage of fixed illustrations. Trojan provided music to both of them.

The score of *The Merry Circus* is actually credited also to Jan Rychlík, who composed two jazz-flavored pieces; Trojan composed four more (Vičar 1989: 124). They mostly function as an accompaniment to circus numbers; the short has, in fact, no unitary narrative arc but consists of a succession of attractions (trained animals, acrobats, clowns) applauded by an audience, also made of paper cut-outs. So, the music tries to replicate a circus experience, by providing a separate piece for each attraction. The pieces often borrow classic atmospheres from the circus tradition; most prominently, at the beginning of the film they pay homage to a world-renowned composition that became indissolubly attached to circus shows, the 1897 *Vjezd gladiátorů*, or *Einzug der Gladiatoren* (*The Entrance of the Gladiators*), a work by a bohemian musician, Julius Ernst Wilhelm Fučík (1872–1916).

Even though the music is divided into independent episodes, there are still elements of general consistency to it. For example, the sound of a fair organ is repeatedly featured, for added realism to a soundtrack that uses also sound effects (like the applause from the audience, or the voices of the clowns) to recreate a stylized circus program. Trojan adds to the timbrical texture also an electric piano; this contamination between traditional and electronic instruments was going to be reprised and expanded on in the concert suites for accordion and chamber ensemble (1960), and for accordion and electrophonic accordion (*Cirkusová suita*, 1980), that the famous accordionist Milan Bláha (1927–2015) compiled after the music of *The Merry Circus*, with the permission of the composer.

The short has no dialogue, but the silent film aesthetic developed by Trnka and Trojan in their previous features is here not in use; the music is always to be understood as diegetic, as proven by the presence of musical instruments on screen (and even of a monkey conductor), but also by revealing synchronies that reinforce the sensation of a link between the sounds and the events. For example, at the end of the short, the incident that comically disrupts the balancing act of a trained bear comes from a bass drum pedal that breaks down, thus stopping the music. The *circus* style used in the score is in good accordance with the narrative context and with Trojan's own attitude towards folk repertoires.

O ZLATÉ RYBCE (THE GOLDEN FISH, 1951)

The music is scarce, in *The Golden Fish*: the most prominent role is in fact assigned to the narrating voice of Jan Werich, a major actor, playwright, and writer. Trnka collaborated with him again in a later short film (*Dva mrazíci, The Two Ice Spirits*, 1954, with music by Ilja Hurník), in the three shorts of the series *Dobrý voják Švejk* (*The Good Soldier Svejk*, 1955) and in two live-action productions: *Císařův pekař – Pekařův císař* (*The Emperor's Baker – The Baker's Emperor*, Martin Frič, 1951; music by Julius Kalaš; Trnka did the costume design), and *Byl jednou jeden král...* (*Once Upon a Time There Was a King...*, Bořivoj Zeman, 1954; music by Trojan; Trnka was art director). Trojan was supposed to work with Werich also in *The Emperor's Baker – The Baker's Emperor*, and he actually started to write a song on Werich's lyrics; however, as the whole film crew changed after a disagreement between Werich and the original director, Jiří Krejčík, Trojan left the production (Vičar 1989: 124). Trnka respected Werich, but on at least one occasion he expressed criticism towards him: in his letter of encouragement to Trojan, on the occasion of the composer's creative crisis during the production of *Old Czech Legends* (see Chapter 2), he mentioned that Werich, "genuinely gifted by God,* […] did not overcome his artistic crisis,† […] he has the talents of an artist, but he has no artist's heart"‡ (Vičar 1989: 105).

Trnka's storytelling in *The Golden Fish* is based on a montage of still drawings, as if to convey the feeling of looking at pictures from a storybook, or, better, from the board of a traveling storyteller, given the presence of a continuous narrative voice. The idea of making a film out of stills anticipates Chris Marker's *La Jetée* (1962), even though the visual style, based on drawings with stark contrasts between light and shadows that make them resemble wood engravings, is profoundly different. The source of the film is once again a popular fairytale, *The Fisherman and His Wife* by the Brothers Grimm; however, Trnka probably refers also to the 1833 Russian version by Aleksandr Sergeevič Puškin. It tells of a fisherman who catches a talking fish that claims to be an enchanted prince; the man releases the creature, but his wife later commands him to go back and ask the fish the granting of a wish in exchange for his freedom. The fisherman complies, but his wife demands more and more wishes, until she wants to become equal to God. At that point, all the effects from the previous wishes disappear and the two find themselves back where they started, in their old, poor house, which is actually a large, empty vinegar bottle.

Werich's voice is sometimes accompanied by sound effects related to the events depicted (wind, waves, bells), with an overall scarcity of music: after the opening title, accompanied by a short orchestral piece where the woodwind seem to imitate birds, with trills and descending third intervals (that mimic cuckoo calls), music returns only during the sequence dedicated to the transformation of the fisherman's wife into a popess. A female vocalizing chorus is introduced, while many people are shown kneeling

---

* "Skutečně nadaný od Boha."
† "Nepřemohl svoji krizi uměleckou."
‡ "Má nadání umělce, ale nemá srdce umělce."

before the woman; however, the accompaniment and the harmony mischievously set the tone of the piece very far from a religious context, giving to it the flavor of 1930s swing. In conclusion, Trojan's contribution to *The Golden Fish* is short and ironically detached from the content (a story about a fish is introduced by music featuring bird imitations; a solemn celebration is accompanied by light dance music); however, this might not be a sign of a lack of interest in the film on behalf of the composer, but instead a strategy to reinforce the pungent, tongue-in-cheek sarcasm of the narration by Trnka and Werich.

The Golden Fish is the first film by Trnka that makes pervasive use of an actor's extradiegetic voice; as such, it testifies to a growing interest of the director in this narrative device that, in his work, was slowly taking over the silent film aesthetic he previously preferred. The transition to the new set of audiovisual strategies centered around the narrating voice was destined to culminate in *Old Czech Legends*.

STARÉ POVĚSTI ČESKÉ (OLD CZECH LEGENDS, 1953)

The 1953 film *Old Czech Legends* might be considered a peak and a turning point in the collaboration between Trnka and Trojan. First of all, the chosen theme explicitly addressed the continuing interest of the two creators in Czech folk heritage. It happened before, as in *The Czech Year*; however, Trnka had never before embedded such a deep continuity between a film's content and the sources that set a standard in the preservation of Czech cultural heritage, like the texts by Cosmas of Prague, the most ancient Czech historian (12th century), or the renowned book by Alois Jirásek *Ancient Bohemian Legends* (1894), that was actually the main reference for the film. The visuals of the film were modeled after famous paintings about episodes of ancient Czech history, by Josef Mánes (1820–1871) and Mikoláš Aleš (1852–1913), in order to connect with the most popular impressions the audience had about the past of their nation (Boillat 1974: 510). Those references resulted in a different appearance for Trnka's puppets: their builds became more monumental;

their faces, more geometric and blockier than usual; and a severe and ancestral composure was added to their usual dreamy gaze. Hames (2009: 191–192) reported that "Blažena Urgošiková argues that the film marks a fundamental metamorphosis in his work. In comparison with previous works, where the puppets manifested fragility and charm, the puppets in *Old Czech Legends* 'are monumentally dramatic and tragic, more individualized; their countenance expresses their character, the inner essence of the represented person.'" The film is probably the final expression of a need for change that Trnka meditated on over the years. All the several projects that the director considered, before he chose the film based on Jirásek's book, testify to a search for innovative solutions and unusual subject matter: first a *Don Quijote*, then a film on the Hussite Wars,* another one on David and Goliath, and finally a mixed technique feature (half animated, half live-action) on the life of Matěj Kopecký. The final choice of *Old Czech Legends* was partly due to pressure from the government, who wanted a film based on Czech myths (Servant 2009: 14). More specifically, Trnka's film was included in a state instrumentalization of Jirásek's life and works, intended to celebrate the historical roots of the socialist Czech culture. The so-called *Jiráskovská akce* (*Action Jirásek*) was launched on November 10, 1948, by the President of the Republic, Klement Gottwalt, and his minister, Zdeněk Nejedlý; it resulted in the opening of a museum dedicated to the author and a new edition of Jirásek's books. The first volume was *Ancient Bohemian Legends* (Sayer 2000: 298–299). According to Derek Sayer, "Jiří Trnka was not representative of those who sought to transform Jirásek into a contemporary figure (though, perhaps, he succeeded better than most)" (Sayer 2000: 300). The theme of the government's limitation of an artist's free will was going to be at the core of Trnka's final work, *The Hand*.

---

* Trnka actually had a chance to give an artistic interpretation of this historical subject, by working as art director for the live-action trilogy of feature films *Jan Hus* (1954), *Jan Žižka* (1955), and *Proti všem* (*Against All*, 1956), all directed by Otakar Vávra.

The film was subdivided into small episodes, as *The Czech Year*; each part actually corresponds to a chapter in Jirásek's book, paralleling thus its literary structure. The six parts, from the beginning of the book, are however thematically interrelated and build a unitary arc. The first story is that of the patriarch Čech (*O praotci Čechovi, On the Patriarch Čech*) who leads his people in the Bohemian territories and helps them settle at the foot of the sacred hill Říp. The legend is narrated in a flashback, because the film actually opens with Čech's funeral. The second part (*O Bivojovi, On Bivoj*) deals with the reign of princess Libuše, the youngest daughter of Krok, Čech's successor. An old traveling poet sings about the ferocious boar that plagues their kingdom; however, the animal is captured, brought to the castle of Vyšehrad, and killed by the brave hunter Bivoj. In the third episode (*O Libuši a Přemyslovi, On Libuše and Přemysl*), Libuše settles a dispute between two brothers for the ownership of a land; one of the two, though, despises the fact that a man should be ruled by a woman. In order to preserve the royal authority, Libuše decides to get married: she chooses a humble farmer she saw in a vision, Přemysl. He is found, brought to Libuše, and made a prince; he vows to rule with humility and firmness, always remembering his modest origins. The episode of the war of the young women (*O dívčí válce*) follows: Libuše dies and some court maids leave the kingdom, despising the return of the power in the hand of men. The proud noblemen Ctirad and his servant deride Vlasta, the leader of the women; she decides to take her vengeance by having Ctirad seduced by Šárka. The young man finds the girl tied to a tree, pretending to have been punished for opposing Vlasta; Ctirad falls in love with her, but is then induced to drink too much hydromel, thus falling asleep. He and his companions wake up prisoner to Vlasta and her warriors; however, other men arrive to help, and a battle starts. Trnka concludes the episode with a rapturous dance sequence that marks a reconciliation between men and women; instead of the bloody repression of the women found in Jirásek's book, it is closer to Cosmas's version of the episode (Servant 2009: 22).

The next part (*O Horymírovi*, *On Horymír*) is about the reign of Křesomysl, the fifth king that succeeded Libuše and Přemysl. It mainly deals with the legendary hero Horymír, who warns Křesomysl against the greedy fascination that farmers have for the gold they extract from the land, forgetting everything about their crops. The goldsmiths are offended by Horymír's warnings and send mercenaries to sack his house; however, Horymír has already been sabotaging the gold mines by filling them with rocks. The king sentences Horymír to death; the hero, as a last wish, asks to ride his white horse one last time. He manages to leap over the walls of the castle and flee beyond a river. The sixth and final episode (*O Lukcé válce*, *On the War of the Lučans*) takes place several years later. The kingdom is ruled by the weak and fearful Neklan; the neighboring Lučans people are about to start a war. All seems lost, but suddenly news comes that the king of Bohemia will wear his armor and lead his army. The Bohemians win, but their king gets killed; as they remove his helmet, they see that they were not led by the cowardly Neklan, but by a brave young man named Čestmír.

Trnka himself acknowledged the remarkable differences existing between *Old Czech Legends* and his earlier films:

> Until now […] everything in our puppet films was played out in a poetic way: we had yet to find how to express the action in a dramatic and epic form. It was only with *Old Czech Legends* that we mastered this issue. Heroism and patriotic lyrism, quite difficult to express in any artistic field, were by no means scarce in this film, and it was sometimes hard to avoid making the pathetic too loud. The development of the action is here faster than in all my previous films, and I see [a] progress in this. The crowd scenes were a first for us, too: to create them in a puppet film without causing great confusion was very difficult. The same goes for the spoken commentary and dialogues:

it was the first time we used words and we devised several ways to do so.*

(TRNKA IN ZANOTTO 1969: 22–23)

The last point mentioned by Trnka was of pivotal importance in sight of Trojan's collaboration: Trnka decided to take advantage of sounds and recorded dialogue, giving voice to the puppets; and those were speaking voices, and not just singing, by adult actors – no more children. The audiovisual role of the music had to change in a quite radical way. Trnka himself knew this would be a challenging task for Trojan:

> The musical score posed serious problems to the composer, Václav Trojan. There was a need for ancient Czech music imbued with the pathetic character of the heroes, and artistically reconstructing, in some moments, the authentic music of those times. As far as the sound was concerned, we tried to stylize it to avoid any disturbance to the stylization of the various sequences and to the whole of the episodes. From this point of view, *Old Czech Legends* was the hardest film I had ever done until that point.†

(TRNKA IN ZANOTTO 1969: 24)

---

* "Sinora [...] nei nostri film di marionette avevamo risolto tutto in modo poetico: non avevamo ancora trovato il modo d'esprimere l'azione sotto una forma drammatica ed epica. È solo con *Vecchie leggende céche* che ci siamo resi padroni di questo problema. L'eroismo e il lirismo patriottico, che sono una cosa difficile in tutti i campi dell'arte, non erano certo scarsi in questo film, ed 'stato arduo evitare che il patetico diventasse talora troppo chiassoso. Lo svolgimento dell'azione vi è più rapido che in tutti i miei film precedenti, ed in ciò io scorgo un progresso. Le scene di massa sono pure state una novità per noi: realizzarle in un film di marionette senza rischiare di provocare una gran confusione è stato molto difficile. Così pure per quanto riguarda il commento parlato e i dialoghi: è la prima volta che abbiamo utilizzato le parole ed abbiamo escogitato diversi metodi per farlo."

† "La partitura musicale [...] ha posto dei gravi problemi al compositore Vaclav Trojan. Occorreva creare una antica musica céca che possedesse il carattere patetico degli eroi e, in certi punti, ricostituire artisticamente la musica autentica d'allora. Per ciò che concerne il suono, s'è dovuto stilizzarlo in modo tale che non turbasse la stilizzazione delle varie sequenze e l'insieme degli episodi. Da questo punto di vista, *Vecchie leggende céche* è stato il film più difficile ch'io abbia girato sinora."

Trojan confirmed and integrated Trnka's observations:

> I have always had in mind that it was a puppet film. I know from experience that puppets cannot tolerate an intellectual musical language, in other words what we call a great sonata form, symphonic music, and so on. On the other hand, the subject was serious, even monumental. I am convinced that only Janáček could have mastered this task. However, Janáček is no more, so I humbly tried to do it. I cannot say how I did it myself, but I think that if someone dared to write a symphony on this subject, that would have been wrong. Even if somebody tried it by following the tradition of Smetana, that would have not been better, because of the arcane and barbarous appearance of Trnka's puppets. There was no choice but to create new, fitting music.*
>
> (TROJAN IN VIČAR 1989: 126–127)

That act of creation was by no means easy. At the time of *Old Czech Legends*, Trojan was under pressure. His artistic stature had been well recognized in the Czech territory; his music for *Prince Bajaja* won a national award in 1950; however, at the 2nd plenary meeting of the Czechoslovak composer, in 1951, Trojan risked the accusation of formalism, one of the most dangerous allegations that could come to an artist under the Soviet regime. The term was used to identify music whose meaning was entirely determined by its form, without any reference to real life and contemporary

---

* "Stále jsem měl na mysli, že jde o loutkový film. Vím ze zkušenosti, že loutky nesnesou intelektuální hudební vyjádření, jinými slovy to, čemu říkáme velká sonátová forma, symfonická hudba a podobně. Na druhé straně šlo tu o námět závažný, ba monumentální. Jsem přesvědčen, že jediný Janáček mohl tento úkol zvládnout. Ale Janáček není a já jsem se o to pokorně pokusil. Nemohu sám říci, jak se mi to podařilo, ale domnívám se, že kdyby se někdo odvážil psát symfonii na toto téma, že by to dopadlo špatně. Také kdyby se o to někdo pokusil v tradici Smetanově, nedopadlo by to lépe vzhledem k archaickým a barbarizujícím postavičkám loutek Trnkových. Nezbývalo, než vymýšlet novou, přiléhavou hudbu."

society. Trojan was spared this humiliation thanks to positive remarks by the Russian composer Dmitrij Borisovič Kabalevskij, that pointed out how actually the integration between Trojan's music and Trnka's direction was so deep that the audience usually forgot that the players were puppets, receiving instead an impression comparable to that of real-life actors (Vičar 1989: 122).

The production circumstances added more complications to Trojan's professional moment. The previous feature, *Bajaja*, had already put to test the composer's resourcefulness; the production was in fact slowed down in early 1950, by the relocation of Trnka's studio from the Chourových houses to the Bartolomějská street in the Prague Old Town. Then, in June, a fire destroyed 1,500 meters of finished film (Vičar 1989: 120). The set deadline was not postponed, though, because the film had to be presented at the upcoming Karlovy Vary festival; Trojan had only one month to compose his score, working at an exhausting pace. Trnka tried his best to avoid excessive stress of his collaborator and friend but remained firm in his requirements; the same happened for *Old Czech Legends*, even though the production schedule was less tight. A further set of difficulties arose because of a fundamental difference in the interpretation of the film between the director and the composer. Trojan's merry and positive artistic outlook did not adapt well to the somber new style that Trnka was exploring; in fact, the composer was probably still seeing the world of puppetry as something to be imbued with an infantile sensibility. After all, he confirmed that this was for him yet another "puppet film," as noted above, not to be burdened with an excessively "intellectual" language. The presence of adult voices, and the overall tone and visual style, showed that Trnka differed on this point. In light of this artistic struggle, it is maybe not that surprising that Trojan never created any concert piece inspired by *Old Czech Legends*, while he did so abundantly with the other four feature films he scored for Trnka.

Trojan, anyway, could still relate very well to the folk undertones of the narration. In fact, he elaborated on those elements by reimagining the sound of ancient Czech instruments. He knew that the historical sources, in this respect, are almost verging on the non-existent; so, he evoked a sense of time-distance by using in unusual combinations the electric piano, the organ, the harp, and various percussion instruments including the Sobot, an instrument Trojan himself invented, in an attempt to recover an ancestral sound from Czech lore: it was made of wooden planks spanning one octave. Trojan also tried to create an authentic *folk* feeling by inserting references to actual Czech popular songs in the score, as he already did in *The Emperor's Nightingale*: for example, he alludes to the melodic profile of the song *Proč, kalino, v struze stojíš?* (*Why do you stand in a brook, plum tree*) in the melodies of the venerable hill Říp and of the mythical princess Libuše (Vičar 2005: 46).

In other cases, though, Trojan did not find a connection with the film scenes. When this happened, Trnka did not force him to come up with some idea but preferred to avoid the use of music altogether, in favor of dialogue and sound effects. Such was the case with a key scene in the film, the battle in the concluding segment of *On the War of the Lučans*. According to Vičar (1989: 127), Trojan did not find a way to connect his sensibility with the war scene, and so he had no music ready when the delivery deadline came; Trnka thus adopted a sound accompaniment based on an orchestration of impactful effects (shouts, animal calls, bells, blasts, and blows), organized so as to convey an emphasized and stylized war atmosphere based on realistic elements. The tension he achieved was compared by some critics to that of the battle on the ice from *Александр Невский* (*Aleksandr Nevskij*, Sergej Michajlovič Ėjzenštejn, 1938) (Zanotto 1969: 24, 27); however, whilst in Trnka the images mostly dialogued with sound effects, with Trojan's music entering only to provide a doleful commentary to the aftermath of the fight, Ėjzenštejn's film mostly relied upon the music by Sergej Sergeevič Prokof'ev to complement and enhance the screen action. The fact that Trnka's scene, devoid of music, was compared to one of the most exemplary moments in the history of film music, suggests the extent of the competence that Trnka developed in the use of sound effects; at the same time, it tells how far Trnka had traveled from his earlier ideas about the aesthetics of puppet plays and silent pantomime. Furthermore, the comparison proves that Trnka's new style could achieve a poignant intensity even without the constant presence of Trojan's music. In the overall design of Trnka's narration, music was apparently shifting towards an underscoring function; it was not deemed to be mere decoration, but its role would no more be that of the sole, privileged interlocutor to the visual rhythms. Synchronies and punctuations were now assigned to recorded effects; the music retained anyway an important purpose, as signifier of emotions and atmospheres. In sound studies, the word *atmosphere* is connected to the concept of *ambient sound*: "The site-specific background sound component that provides locational atmosphere and spatial information in both film and sound art production" (Chattopadhyay 2017). Trnka's films used a mono mix, so an actual spatialization of sound was not feasible; however, effects like reverberations, echoes, or intensity variations were applied to give the illusion of distance or proximity to the listener. This became more evident in the following films by the two authors, and evidently so in their last full-length feature, *A Midsummer Night's Dream*. The creation of an atmosphere, in particular, took over the most conspicuous and original audiovisual function that Trojan's music had before: the replacement of dialogues and effects with interdiegetic ambivalence. With its new atmospheric value, Trojan's music found a way to retain a connection with the diegetic space, but on a different premise: the audience would no more receive synchronized simulations of voices and noises, but a musical rendering that communicates the physical extension and emotional character of an ambient.

In *Old Czech Legends*, though, this atmospheric function is still embryonal; it appears seldom, and mostly in the sung parts. For example, in the scene where the hunter Bivoj brings the boar he fought to his people, a choir celebrates his brave deed and the liberation from a deadly danger: the voices change their intensity and reverberation in accordance with the point of view and the supposed closeness of the audience to the diegetic music. Just before this scene, a similar spatial use of a tenor solo is used when Bivoj is shown walking in the snow while singing; apart from the reverb and the intensity variations, responding to the distance of the character from the point of view (Figure 4.5), his singing gets interrupted midway several times, as he finds the track of the boar, suggesting thus the diegetic nature of the sound; he also attempts shortly to reprise his song to calm down the wild animal, just before getting brutally attacked.

The fact that the *atmospheric* value of Trojan's music finds a way into the film through diegetic singing is meaningful. In a sound film, the human voice is the soundtrack element that gets the most of the audience's attention: a feature that Chion called *vococentrisme* (Chion 1982: 15–16). As Trnka introduced dialogues and his aesthetics abandoned the *silent film* setting, where all sounds are of equal importance, music was rendered secondary in respect to the spoken word. So, the attribution of an atmospheric/spatial

FIGURE 4.5   Bivoj in the snow; still from *Staré pověsti české* (*Old Czech Legends*, 1953). (From Národní filmový archiv/National Film Archive [NFA], Prague. With permission.)

value to vocal compositions ensured that this function would fall into the main attentive focus of the audience. Moreover, the spatial effects reinforce the notion that the music is coming from the universe of the film, consolidating thus the link between the voices and the unmoving faces of the puppets; the affirmation of this link was of crucial importance, in light of the previous films by Trnka, where puppets did not talk at all, or sang with children's voices (with the only exception of Bajaja). Furthermore, the clear attribution of the vocal music to the on-screen action recovered the frequent diegetic value that music had had in the previous features by Trnka, thus smoothing the transition to the new aesthetics.

In *Old Czech Legends*, Trojan kept anyway something of his previous synchronic approach to puppet music; for instance, he illustrates the sudden flashes of lightning bolts in the sky with short passages given to the shrill timbre of the piccolo flute. That synchrony, however, does not seem to be a substitute for a sound effect (lightning does not emit sound; it could appear together with thunder, that however might not be effectively suggested by the high-pitched notes of a piccolo); instead, it seems to provide a musical equivalent to the sudden movement on screen, embodying thus a Mickey-Mousing moment, more than an interdiegetic function.

In conclusion, *Old Czech Legends* testifies to the apparition of a substantial artistic divide in the aesthetic views of Trnka and Trojan. However, the introduction of an *atmospheric* function of music, with spatial implications, created a balance between the older silent film strategies by Trojan and the newer sound film approach by Trnka, centered on spoken dialogues and sound effects.

JAK STAŘEČEK MĚNIL, AŽ VYMĚNIL (HOW THE OLD MAN TRADED IT ALL AWAY, 1953)

Just like had happened after *Prince Bajaja*, after the completion of his feature *Old Czech Legends* Trnka dedicated himself to short films. *How the Old Man Traded It All Away* was another story illustrated with still images, in the fashion of *The Golden Fish*. The source is a folk tale collected by the ethnomusicologist František Bartoš (1837–1906): a peasant saves the life of a merchant and receives a gold bar from him. He trades it for a horse, then he keeps trading and gets an ox, a ram, a pig, and finally a small ornament for his wife. However, he loses it; but when he returns home, his wife is not angry; she is just happy that he had returned safely.

Again, the soundtrack is mainly occupied by a narrative voice, provided by Růžena Nasková; Trojan's music appears principally during the opening titles. The short composition featured there sounds like a small neoclassical overture, whose main theme has a mocking and high-spirited attitude, thanks to the use of a *staccato* fast passage by a solo bassoon. The theme occasionally returns in a few moments of the film, making witty remarks on the misadventures of the old peasant. There is also a recurring flute passage, though, opened by a very simple motif (G-A-B-C-D) that recalls that of Papageno's pan flute calls in his aria *Der Vogelfänger bin ich ja* (*The Bird Catcher I Am Indeed*), from Wolfgang Amadeus Mozart's *Die Zauberflöte* (*The Magic Flute*). *How the Old Man Traded It All Away* confirms the establishment of a preferential role of extradiegetic commentary for Trojan's music in Trnka's films, while substantiating once more the importance of neoclassicism in the composer's style.

DOBRÝ VOJÁK ŠVEJK (THE GOOD SOLDIER ŠVEJK, 1954–1955)

Trnka did not collaborate with Trojan, but with Ilja Hurník (1922–2013), a renowned composer and essayist, in the next short he directed, *The Two Ice Spirits*: yet another experimental foray, where Trnka mixed together puppets and animated drawings to bring alive the main players, two transparent, ghost-like snowmen. Trnka resumed his work with Trojan when he returned to his favorite medium, puppet animation, in a work that is sometimes mentioned as a full-length feature but is actually a series of three shorts with the same main character: the Good Soldier Švejk, a famous protagonist from an anti-militarist novel by the anarchic journalist Jaroslav Hašek (1883–1923). Originally born as a series of short stories in 1912, and then planned as a six-volume work, *Osudy dobrého vojáka Švejka za světové války* (*The Fateful Adventures of the Good Soldier Švejk During the World War*) was left incomplete, at just three volumes, because of the untimely death of the author in 1923. It chronicled the travels of Švejk, a soldier during the First World War, who appears to be a simpleton but is actually wisely disillusioned about life: his optimistic and pacific disposition often exposes the nonsenses of war, as well as the hypocrisy and weakness of his superiors. Hašek did not live to see the overwhelming success of his character; in 1926, for example, even Erwin Piscator and Bertolt Brecht adapted the novel for the stage, with the participation of the painter George Grosz; Brecht returned to Švejk in 1945, with the play *Schweyk im Zweiten Weltkrieg* (*Švejk in the Second World War*). Hašek's book became the most translated in the whole of Czech literature; it even influenced the Czech language, which today includes the words *švejkovina* (*act like a Švejk*), *švejkovat* (*in Švejk's manner*), and *švejkárna* (*a military foolishness*).

Trnka's take on Švejk was thus just one among many others; however, he differed in the fact that, thanks to the animated medium, he had a chance to bring to the screen characters designed after the renowned illustrations that accompanied the Švejk novels, by Josef Lada (1887–1957), a self-taught caricaturist and close friend of Hašek. Trnka's film was released two years prior to a live-action film on the same subject (*Dobrý voják Švejk*, *The Good Soldier Švejk*, Karel Steklý, 1957), but it was not the first theatrical adaptation of Hašek's novel: it was preceded by two films by Karel Lamač (*Dobrý voják Švejk*, *The Good Soldier Švejk*; *Švejk na frontě*, *Švejk at the Front*, 1926), as well as by *Švejk v ruském zajetí* (*Švejk in Russian captivity*, Svatopluk Innemann, 1926), *Švejk v civilu* (*Švejk as a civilian*, Gustav Machatý, 1927) and *Dobrý voják*

Švejk (*The Good Soldier Švejk*, Martin Frič,* 1931). The last one was a sound film (the others were silent), with a soundtrack that included several songs.

Trnka's shorts continued this film tradition with a sound film approach, coherently with the preference demonstrated by the director in his previous recent works. So, the puppets were again dubbed, like in *Old Czech Legends*, while Jan Werich's voice-over provided the narration. Moreover, the dubbing was partly synchronized with the movements of articulated jaws, as in the case of Švejk's superiors; that unusual detail, for Trnka's standards, was not however added in for realism, but to achieve a caricatural effect. During the dialogues and the interventions of the narrator no music at all was heard. This choice actually favored a closer restitution of Hašek's surrealism, that was often based on verbal interactions destabilized by Švejk's candidness, as well as double-entendres (Parrott 1982: 91): dialogue, in the novel, has an importance comparable to that of a theatrical play (Cosentino in Hašek 2016: xvi). The *Švejk* series constituted thus the culmination of Trnka's transition to the sound film aesthetic, and the strongest departure from his pristine ideals about the best soundscape for puppet plays. Trnka was aware of this, and he actually regretted the outcome:

> While working on this film, we found out that the way in this direction has limits and limits, because it really makes no sense to penetrate with the technique of puppet film into an area in which live actors can better express the intention and ideas of the author. Švejk was a valuable lesson for me and my colleagues. It allowed us to go through one of the many creative ways of the puppet film, to the end of this task. What we have kept in mind in our reflections on

---

* Trnka collaborated with Frič, as costume designer, in the 1947 film *Čapkovy povídky* (*Čapek's Tales*); he had the same mansion in a previous unfinished production by Frič, *Černí myslivci* (*Gamekeepers in Black*, 1944).

new thematic areas and the creative possibilities of puppet film is an even closer connection between the image and the acting of animated puppets with music. In my next films, I would like to reserve a lot more space and more importance to music than in Švejk ....*

(TRNKA IN VIČAR 1989: 131; 134)

In the *Švejk* shorts, however, music is not irrelevant; on the contrary, Trojan's work significantly contributed to their satirical vein. The composer opted for a score mostly based on a pre-existing repertoire, rather than writing new music (occasionally accompanied by some folk song quotations, as he previously used to do): he selected pieces strongly connected with the time setting of the story, and especially with the Austro-Hungarian Empire. He collected forty-one works (Vičar 1989: 134) pertinent to the moods and circumstances of the film and used them in a mostly antiphrastic manner. For example, each short is opened by the famous *Radetzky-Marsch* (1848) by Johann Strauss I; Trojan overplays its military undertones by adding in thunderous interventions of bass drums and percussion instruments. The apparition of Švejk coincides with the beginning of the trio of the march, its contrasting middle section; at that point, Trojan deviates from Strauss's score and blends it with the melodic line of a licentious folk song, *Má roztomilá Baruško* (*My Cute Baruch*). The association with the lazy and desecrating *Švejk*, as well as several parodistic dissonances introduced by Trojan in the *contaminated* trio,

---

* "Při práci na tomto filmu jsme se přesvědčili, že cesta tímto směrem má své hranice a meze, nebot opravdu nemá smysl pronikat s technikou loutkového filmu stůj co stůj do oblasti, v níž mohou živí herci lépe vyjádřit záměr a myšlenky autora. – Švejk byl pro mne a mé spolupracovníky svým způsobem cenným poučením. Umožnil nám projít při řešení tohoto úkolu jednou z mnoha tvůrčích cest loutkového filmu až na samý její konec. – To, co máme ve svých úvahách o nových tematických oblastech a tvůrčích možnostech loutkového filmu již několik let neustále na mysli, je ještě těsnější sepětí obrazu a hry oživlých loutek s hudbou. – Ve svých příštích filmech bych chtěl hudbě vyhradit opět mnohem více místa a větší důležitost, než jako tomu bylo například ve Švejkovi...."

deflate the pompous attitude of the piece and make it a musical equivalent to the satirical stance of the *Švejk* narrative: it reveals the vacuity and fragility of the Austrian military power during the Great War.

The association between Švejk and the *Radetzky-Marsch* was so effective that it was literally reprised in the 1986 ten-episode remake/sequel of the puppet films by Trnka, directed by one of his animators and closest collaborators, Stanislav Látal.

The musical repertoire individuated by Trojan was an eclectic one; it included the popular song *Lístečku dubový* (*The Oak Leaf*), *Cikánko ty krásná* (*Beautiful Gypsy Girl*), by Karel Vacek, the patriotic German song *Die Wacht am Rhein* (*The Watch on the Rhine*), by Karl Wilhelm, the galop *Na motoru* by František Kmoch and *Da geh ich zu Maxim* (*I Go Now to Maxim's*) from Franz Lehár's *Die lustige Witwe* (*The Merry Widow*). Such extensive use of pre-existing music was a first, for Trojan; it was, however, an incisive way to address a narration mainly based on parody. Trojan approached the Austro-Hungarian repertoire with a similarly parodistic intent, centered around the discrepancy between the familiarity of the audience with the featured pieces and the unexpected use of such music in the film.

KUŤÁSEK A KUTILKA JAK RÁNO VSTÁVALI (KUŤÁSEK AND KUTILKA WOKE UP IN THE MORNING, 1955)

Kuťásek and Kutilka Woke Up in the Morning was the last short film Trnka and Trojan created together, before Trnka's two-year hiatus from directing. Trnka continued to work in cinema anyway with other roles, in that period; for instance, he returned to live-action cinema and, just like he did for the 1954 *Once Upon a Time There Was a King...*, he was costume designer and art director for the three films of the Hussite trilogy by Otakar Vávra (1954–1956). He also designed puppets and scenes for puppet films directed by his colleagues, like the second short from the Kuťásek and Kutilka series, *Kuťásek a Kutilka na pouti* (*Kuťásek and Kutilka at the Fair*, Stanislav Látal, 1955), *Spejbl na stopě* (*Spejbl on the Trail*, Břetislav

Pojar, 1956), and *Paraplíčko* (*The Little Umbrella*, Břetislav Pojar, 1957). *Spejbl on the trail* testifies to a renewed interest by Trnka and his collaborators in the classic puppet performances by Skupa, maybe as a reaction to the great distance that had progressively separated Trnka's style from that of his mentor; in 1955, Trnka had already revived Skupa's characters in the short *Cirkus Hurvínek* (*Hurvínek's Circus*; music by Jan Rychlík).

During those years, Trojan kept a position as a teacher at the Academy of Performing Arts in Prague, while writing for radio, television, and theatrical plays, providing music for shows ideated and interpreted by renowned authors and actors like Jan Werich and Vlasta Burian (1891–1962). Among his production of radio music from the 1950s, it is worth mentioning a version of Shakespeare's *A Midsummer Night's Dream*, directed by Josef Bezdíček, that premiered on June 25, 1950; Trojan had already written incidental music for a theatrical staging of the play in 1943, at the Urania Theater. Some of the music from the 1943 version was featured in the 1950 production, that remained, however, a distinct and original work; when Trojan composed for Trnka's 1959 film based on the same source, he did not use any music from his two previous scores. In 1957, the concerts and publications that celebrated Trojan's 50th birthday confirmed his recognition as one of the leading Czech composers of his time.

Kuťásek and Kutilka Woke Up in the Morning is a small film centering around two hand puppets that starred in popular tv shows for children, created by the pedagogue Josef Pehr. Because of the nature of the puppets, the film does not feature animation: the characters move thanks to unseen puppeteers under the stage, as they interact with a real actor, Pehr himself. So, the film can be considered a live-action one, where the protagonist is Pehr, more than the puppets (that do not speak and just react to the actor's words). Notwithstanding the constant presence of speech, the films feature more music than the previous films by Trnka: Trojan's underscoring, in fact, is here allowed to continue in the background, even when the actor is saying his lines. The score has mostly the function of creating a playful and positive mood; its major comedic strategies rest on the unexpected use of musical sounds. Even in the opening titles, the composer uses solo instruments in tight alternation that pair up low and high pitches echoing each other's melodies, as if one is mocking the other. The strategic use of the several independent soloists reveals its farcical potential when the actor and the puppet embrace instruments on stage and play them: the sounds they make are always wrong, as they are "dubbed" by another instrument. A scene that brings to the extreme this kind of sound humor is that of Pehr trying to wake up Kuťásek: he first blows into a party horn, and we hear a muted trumpet instead. Then he uses a party trumpet, that sounds like a French horn. When he plays the trumpet, the timbre is that of a tuba; and finally, the sound of a muted trumpet returns as Pehr embraces a tuba. But the sound substitutions are not over yet; Pehr visibly snorts out of disappointment, and the sound of a tuba seems to come out of his blown cheeks. This humoristic strategy seems a continuation, with different purposes and premises, of Trojan's typical musical imitations of sound effects in earlier films by Trnka; the mindset that made a violin perform the song of a nightingale is the same behind the disgruntled tuba sound associated with Pehr's grimace. However, the strategy, in the precedent cases, had a lyrical and evocative taste and expressed its full potential thanks to the *interdiegetic* silent film aesthetics, that made the *wrong* sound plausible, as the *real* one was not expected to be heard at all. *Kuťásek and Kutilka Woke Up in the Morning* is instead a sound film, and very clearly so; in this case, then, the sound substitutions play with the expectations of the audience and, by betraying them, they can only result in an invitation to laugh at the *wrong* audiovisual associations. The rest of the score uses short leitmotifs and traditional underscoring; interestingly, Kutilka's leitmotif, B-A-E, is very close to the profile of the *miláčku* call in *Prince Bajaja*. Here, however, it is plainly diatonic (there are no altered notes): so it is devoid of the anguished pathos of its pristine incarnation and retains only a maternal placidness, signified by its descending arc. After all, Kutilka is partly a maternal figure who collaborates with Pehr when it is time to wake up the reluctant Kuťásek.

PROČ UNESCO (WHY UNESCO?, 1958)

Trnka returned to directing in a quite unusual way. The next short film he authored did not feature puppets, but animated drawings. Also, the topic and its treatment were not common for Trnka: a metaphoric celebration of the role of UNESCO in promoting cultural progress and peace, through four parallel stories about a farmer, a fisherman, an inventor, and an artist. From the visual point of view, Trnka adopts here a more decided stylization, that firmly creates a two-dimensional feeling. The opening sequence looks like a homage to the works by Émile Cohl, the father of animated drawings, marked by the continuous metamorphosis of single lines and shapes in a flat, monochromatic space. The rest of the short is instead in color, and while the character design clearly shows the hand of Trnka, the stylization strategies resonate with the trends of international hand-drawn animation at the end of the 1950s: a call to stylization contemporarily (and sometimes independently) came from the works of the United Productions of America (UPA; *Gerald McBoing-Boing*, Robert Cannon, 1950), the early Zagreb School (*Samac*, "The lonely one," Vatroslav Mimica, 1958) and the first short by Bruno Bozzetto (*Tapum! La storia delle armi* [*Tapum!, The History of Weapons*], 1958).

Trojan's music, as Trnka promised after *Švejk*, is restored back to a large audiovisual role: the short film has no dialogues, and a narrator is heard only in the opening and final sequences. There are, anyway, sound effects and moments of silence. The music recovers many of the audiovisual functions it had in earlier works by Trnka and Trojan: the short film feels like a simple anthology of typical strategies the two authors used in the past.

The new compositions by Trojan are mainly catalyzers of moods and emotions; synchronies are however also featured, as when the movement of gears set in motion by the inventor is accompanied by obstinate repetitions of melodic fragments. The *mechanical* effect is not far from that used for the song of the artificial bird in *The Emperor's Nightingale*. The management of single timbres is also carefully tailored to the narration; for example, a melancholic oboe solo is associated with the farmer and his troubles with the weather, while the sound of a mandolin signifies the simple life of the fishermen. Trojan uses again the electric piano, that he previously introduced in *The Merry Circus* and *Kuťásek and Kutilka Woke Up in the Morning*; here he associates it with the creative struggles of the artist. The imaginative rendition of the sound from on-screen instruments is also present when the artist plays a cithara; in this case, the sound is however quite close to the expected one, as the composer assigns it to a harp. At one point the character plays from sheet music, but the printed notes do not correspond at all to those in the soundtrack.

Another musical idea that Trojan reprises from his past works is the creation of an ominous atmosphere with low-pitched sound from timpani and a piano played with the right pedal down, so that the chords overlap amidst long reverberations. The result is at the interface between music and sound effect; it was already featured in the scene of the ghost's apparition in *Old Czech Legends*. In general, the score of *Why UNESCO?* makes the most of Trojan's competence in the use of each single instrument with a dramatic signification; the way the sounds are individualized and characterized gives them a sort of personality, even when there are no strict synchronic and visual associations between a protagonist and an instrument (as it was in the case of the bird and the violin in *The Emperor's Nightingale*).

The only major feature of Trojan's style that seems to be missing in *Why UNESCO?* is the quotation of preexisting music. There are, indeed, folk undertones to the use of the mandolin and in some melodic lines; but there is no direct reference to the popular repertoire. The main theme of the pieces where the whole orchestra plays, at the beginning and at the end, is however strangely similar to the *Promenade* from *Картинки с выставки*

(*Kartinki s vystavki, Pictures at an Exhibition*) by Modest Petrovič Musorgskij. The similarity is maybe a nod to the fact that Trnka's film, just like Musorgskij's piano cycle, is made of separate episodes that are part of a bigger, unitary design.

SEN NOCI SVATOJÁNSKÉ (A MIDSUMMER NIGHT'S DREAM, 1959)

Trnka's fifth and last full-length feature was a continuation of past traditions while breaking new ground at the same time. As for the links with the past, one detail particularly evidences how Trnka wanted *A Midsummer Night's Dream* to restore his pristine vision of puppet animation. The director wanted to go back to the theatrical roots of his art; for this reason, he also considered a puppet version of Wolfgang Amadeus Mozart's singspiel *Bastien und Bastienne.* The project was discarded in favor of the Shakespeare play and, in an almost poetical self-reference, the character of the mischievous Puck was modeled on the puppet the author made during his training with Skupa (see Chapter 2). The film intended also to reinstate the previous audiovisual style by Trnka and Trojan, in a form that the director defined as a "fairy ballet pantomime"* (Vičar 1989: 158).

In terms of cinema heritage, *A Midsummer Night's Dream* continued a tradition of film adaptation, like the 1909 American silent short by Charles Kent and James Stuart Blackton, or the lost 1914 German version by Stellan Rye, *Ein Sommernachtstraum in unserer Zeit.* In 1935, Max Reinhardt and William Dieterle directed an Academy Award-winning take on Shakespeare's comedy, with a soundtrack featuring music by Felix Mendelssohn-Bartholdy, arranged by Erich Wolfgang Korngold. In 1958, the BBC produced a TV version of the play, directed by Rudolph Cartier; however, it can be assumed that Trnka did not have any chance to watch it, also because his animated film stayed in production for about two years before its release. A more meaningful precedent to Trnka's

---

* "Baletně pantomimická féerie."

work is an unfinished 1948 puppet film by Władysław Starewicz: it was widely advertised in Europe but, even though the puppet cast had been completely built, filming never began, because the producer Charles-François de Meduna went bankrupt (Ford and Hammond 2015: 52). The music of Starewicz's feature was to be composed by Georges Auric; the actor Henri Debain was in charge of the synchrony. Trnka's film did not pay direct homage to this unachieved attempt, but it indirectly demonstrated the validity of Starewicz's intuition about having puppets perform a work by Shakespeare. The presence of Trojan, moreover, paralleled the involvement of Auric: they were both renowned composers, but by no means specialized in film music only.

Trnka's *A Midsummer Night's Dream* continued a musical tradition, too: the original play inspired about 1,700 compositions (Vičar 2005: 47). In the 1950s, as today, the original play was still almost indissolubly bound to the incidental music by Mendelssohn (1826 and 1842). At the time of Trnka's film, Benjamin Britten was about to turn the comedy into an opera (1960); as for Trojan, he had already composed on this subject twice, in 1943 and 1950 (see above). He would reutilize and rework the music for Trnka's 1959 puppet film in a 1984 pantomime-ballet; for the centenary of the Prague National Theater; and in 1985, after Trojan's demise, the music was used in a ballet film by Vladimír Sís, *Sen noci...* (*The Night's Dream...*).

A Midsummer Night's Dream, however, was not only a perpetuator of a tradition; it was also a film packed with a number of major expressive and technological novelties, for Trnka's standards and Czech cinema as a whole. This is also the reason why, while the film stayed in production for two years, the deadlines were met in a hurry (in this respect, Trojan wrote a meaningful note on the last page of his score: "The end of the torment!"*; Vičar 1989: 162); in fact, the introduced innovations sometimes did not meet the director's expectations and the work had to be discarded

---

* "Konec trápení!"

and started over again. Such was the case for the use of the Eastmancolor process, that generated images more natural and crisper than the Agfacolor Trnka was familiar with (Boček 1965: 225); this choice was connected also to the use of a Cinemascope frame and screen format; however, the film was also shot in a parallel version, with a classic 4:3 screen format (the Academy ratio). It was the first puppet feature in widescreen format; it was also the first Czech film to use a stereophonic soundtrack, an element that allowed for a more defined and convincing use of the *atmospheric* functions of Trojan's music.

Innovations appeared also in the building of the puppets, whose bodies were made of smooth rubber, making their skins more realistic; this also changed the way light defined their fixed facial expressions (light and shadow contrasts were decidedly softer and *dreamier* than in *Old Czech Legends*). The new build also allowed for more complex and expressive movements of hands and fingers. The visual storytelling was renovated too, as Trnka introduced in some scenes a creative splitting of the screen, that took advantage of the wide frame format. Finally, the return to silent pantomime was not only something that harked back to the past, but also a daring and unexpected move, as it required a profound reinvention of the original source, founded on a literary use of words: it sought to create a "Shakespeare without Shakespeare," as Boček put it (1965: 221). Trnka attended to this task with Jiří Brdečka, a regular screenplay collaborator of his; in the end, though, some interventions from a narrator were needed, and these were voiced by Rudolf Pellar. Trnka supervised also foreign dubbed versions; the English one featured Richard Burton as the narrator.

Notwithstanding the difficult work conditions and the pressing deadlines, Trojan remembered his experience with *A Midsummer Night's Dream* as a pleasant one. In particular, the tripartition of the narrative arc, already present in Shakespeare, offered him fertile ground for musical invention: "I can say that this job was true bliss for me. Three worlds – the palace people, the simple artisans, and the gods – provided me with rich inspiration. The gallant

Reinassance themes contrast with comic folk elements. And because I wished the artisans well, these elements were Czech, possibly the tones of Czech Christmas Carols. Finally, there is music of, let us say, a rural character, the voice of the gods and the elements of the earth" (Trojan in Vičar 2005: 48). The storyline elements Trojan evidenced in Trnka and Brdečka's script closely follow the original play: in ancient Greece, Athens is preparing to celebrate the marriage between king Theseus and Hyppolyta, queen of the Amazons. Egeus, father of Hermia, demands the king's judgment in order to settle a controversy about his daughter's engagement; in fact, she was promised to Demetrius, but she is in love with Lysander. Theseus decrees that a vow cannot be broken; as a consequence, Hermia and Lysander flee to the nearby forest. Helena, a girl who is suffering unrequited love for Demetrius, reveals to him where the two fugitives are, hoping for gratitude; they both head to the forest. Meanwhile, a troupe of amateur actors rehearses a play they intend to offer for the royal wedding, about the lovers Pyramus and Thisbe; however, the din in the city forces them to go seek some peace in the forest, too. Said forest is ruled by fairies; Oberon, their king, is in love with Titania, who scorns him. Oberon then orders Puck to go find a magical flower, whose scent induces love at first sight. Puck uses the flower to satisfy his whims: he runs into Demetrius, Lysander, Hermia, and Helena, and makes both men fall for Helena. Moreover, he turns the head of the lead amateur actor, Nick Bottom, into that of a donkey, and he makes Titania fall in love with him. When Oberon finds out about Puck's mischief, he scolds him and restores the order. In the end, a triple marriage is celebrated, as the magical flower unites Helena to Demetrius, and Hermia to Lysander (as well as Titania to Oberon). The amateurs can finally perform their act for Theseus; a curtain closes then, signaling the end of the film and of "Shakespeare's dream."

Trnka conceded only one major deviation from Shakespeare's plot: the play of the amateurs is not laughed at, but is instead professional and deeply emotional, thanks to the magical intervention of Puck, who is amending for his previous bad behavior. This choice is a sign of the high respect Trnka had for popular theater, having himself contributed to one of its expressions (Czech puppetry). This particular choice also let Trojan elaborate on his interest for folk-like music writing: he gave the amateurs a theme that, as quoted above, had some traits of Czech carols; a past equivalent could be found in the *Bethlehem* segment from *The Czech Year*. The use of trills, band-like accompaniments, occasional drones, polytonality, and neoclassical phrasing, all strongly reaffirm a syncretic style typical of Trojan, balanced between cultured writing and popular references. This is not, however, just background music; the amateurs' music triggers also a leitmotif function, as it is heard every time it is needed to signal their relevance to the story. Another leitmotif function is associated with Lysander's theme, that also reintroduces the interdiegetic traits typical of Trnka's past features. The puppet is in fact animated to suggest that he is directly playing the beginning of his theme on his flute; as the action unfolds, however, the music disconnects from his acting and carries on independently, while developing its initial motif (made of two short riffs: E_3-E_4-B_3; $C\#_4$-$G\#_4$-$F\#_4$-B_3). Interestingly, this also bears similarities with some past works by Trojan; several melodies of his were based on very short motifs that insistently circled around a note, with a resulting lilting feeling. The same happened in Bajaja's march, for example: the melodic contour was B_3-A_3-B_3-$G\#_3$-B_3-A_3-B_3-$G\#_3$-B_3-E_4-$F\#_4$-$G\#_4$-$F\#_4$-E_4-B_3. Just like in Lysander's motif, the pivotal note was B.

Another musical idea that restores past audiovisual interrelations between Trojan's music and Trnka's images is the theme of Bottom as a donkey; the woodblock accompaniment has an onomatopoeic value (even though there is no visual synchrony with movement at all), as it recalls the sound of the hoofs of a walking donkey. In addition to that, the blues-like flavor of the piece might be compared with that of the composition *The Frog* from *The Emperor's Nightingale*, which was strongly onomatopoeic, too. A fleeting reference to *The Emperor's Nightingale* might also be contained in the high-pitched violin solo that accompanies the image of a bird, in the sequence that introduces Titania and her fairies.

The onomatopoeic and interdiegetic musical functions are however less pervasively featured than the *atmospheric* ones, that instead elaborate on the developments in the audiovisual style seen in Trnka's films after *Prince Bajaja*. The four-track stereophonic mix of *A Midsummer Night's Dream* permitted a more precise management of the point of hearing; in particular, the soundtrack took advantage of technology to create an illusion of variable depth. The sound seems to be moving in the third dimension, usually with the effect of seeming to move progressively nearer to the audience. The aural distance is further signified by reverberations that create an impression of vast distances or spaces. The scenes in the forest are largely characterized by such aural depth, that add to the eerie dreamlike quality of the setting.

The *atmospheric* disposition of the music in relation to the image that already appeared in *Old Czech Legends* is however different from the one that *A Midsummer Night's Dream* poses. In the former film, the spatial sense mostly reinforced diegetic synchronies between the presence of puppets and their voices; so, this aided the audience in believing that a character (or a group) was actually singing beyond the screen. In *A Midsummer Night's Dream*, instead, the atmospheric function is more radical and intermixed with the interdiegetic and leitmotif ones. That is to say that the music is sometimes associated with the position of a character and it sounds as if it were coming from that place. However, the music is not interpretable as a diegetic sound; there are no visible instruments playing when it is heard, so it is extradiegetic; but it is spatially situated as diegetic. This effect can be clearly appreciated in the scene of the arrival of the amateur actors in the forest; they are seen in the distance from the point of view of Puck and Oberon, who are looking down from above, among the tree branches. The leitmotif of the amateurs starts playing, but at a low volume and with plenty of reverberations: the sensation is that of a sound emanating from the actors themselves, distant from the point of hearing. The same happens to Lysander's theme, as he enters the forest with Hermia. The contradiction between the extradiegetic/leitmotif nature of the music and its diegetic spatial treatment is rendered possible by the pantomimic audiovisual style adopted by Trnka. As in the director's previous silent film aesthetics, the audience here does not have access to a diegetic soundscape, so the music is free to ignore or reference the diegesis at will. The compresence of an extradiegetic quality (the music is a leitmotif played by an orchestra, when there is no orchestra on screen) and a diegetic signal (the music seems to come from a definite place, deep into the film world) is believable and consistent because of the pantomimic premises; it is a new take on the interdiegetic function that adds aural depth as a new variable to its expressive tools.

The atmospheric and spatial feeling in the soundtrack of the film is however also consolidated by use of reverberations that extends beyond music in a strict sense. Especially in the forest scenes, the screen action is immersed in a chain of slow, echoing single notes from wooden percussion instruments, mingled with a droning wind effect. When Puck flies off to the island of the magical flower, the statues there are revealed to be secretly alive because of their constant, reverberating whispers. Incidentally, this story idea seems to introduce a self-reflexive critical joke about puppets and voices in this film: the puppets do not need voices to come alive on screen, as all they need is animation, lighting, and an expressive facial design; however, an unmoving marble statue can be imbued with illusory life if it is associated with a synchronized voice, revealing thus how misleading the synchronic association between images and sounds can be. In general, reverberations and whispers are posed as the founding sound features that orient the spectator in deciphering the unusual audiovisual strategies of the film.

A Midsummer Night's Dream is not, anyway, a purely pantomimic feature, in the fashion of *The Czech Year*. As pointed out above, there is the voice of a narrator; sometimes, moreover, the characters sing, like the puppets of *Old Czech Legends*. In those cases, voices are treated diegetically; while the narrator talks the music is preferably absent, and when the protagonists of the Pyramus and Thysbe play call each other's names, as in the final stage act in front of Theseus, they chant them with no harmonic accordance with the background music. In short, it feels like they cannot hear any music, so their calls are melodically independent from (and in marked contrast to) the orchestral accompaniment. This ambiguous occasional treatment of the pantomimic style adds a quirky touch of uncertainty to the film, in line with the theme of dreaming that pervades it.

There are also extradiegetic orchestral pieces that underscore some scenes in a traditional way, in terms of mainstream film music practice. For example, during the introduction of Titania (and her living mantle, made of dozens of separately-animated small puppet fairies, one of the most remarkable feats ever pulled by Trnka's animators), an orchestral scherzo is heard. It is the only moment in the whole score of this film that closely recalls the most famous musical interpretation of Shakespeare's play, the incidental music by Mendelssohn: specifically, the woodwind writing, the trills and the irregular accents sound like a hybridization (in spirit and feeling only; the notes are different) between the *Scherzo* and the *March of the Elves*.

Among the most remarkable extradiegetic uses of sound in the film, however, there are some peculiar synchronic moments, triggered by strange musical notes that were not part of Trojan's score. They were, in fact, the responsibility of Trnka alone; Vičar (2005: 48) describes them as "musique concrète and electronic sounds." They are played simultaneously to sudden (and aggressive) apparitions of supernatural characters, like the scornful Oberon; they obliterate any other sound and even interrupt music midway. The induced effect of emotional contrast is stark, also because of their plainly artificial nature, very far from the orchestral sound of Trojan's music. Their audiovisual sense is similar to the so-called *stinger* of horror films: an unpleasant, puncturing sound is concentrated in a very short amount of time, in blatant synchrony with the apparition of an unexpected (and mostly unsettling) image. It is curious, to say the least, that Trnka decided to exhibit his personal musical competences in his last feature in such a way; in fact, the need for synchrony of this strategy is contrary to the pantomimic freedom that the rest of the film seems to celebrate. Moreover, the brutal interruptions of music passages feel almost like a gauntlet thrown down to Trojan, in acknowledgment of the aesthetic distance that progressively emerged between the two artists after *Old Czech Legends*. However, the positive dramatic impact that those moments have on the narration disprove this interpretation; *A Midsummer Night's Dream* was, after all, Trnka's reconciliation with Trojan's music, after the preference accorded to words in *The Good Soldier Švejk*. Moreover, Trojan was going to embrace the use of unrealistic electronic sounds himself in the very last score he was to write for Trnka, *The Hand*. Trnka's *stingers* might thus be read in light of the productive contradictions that populate the audiovisual treatment of *A Midsummer Night's Dream*. If a negative critical implication is to be found in the boldly contrasting attitudes of those sounds, that might not be directed towards the relationship between Trnka and Trojan, but towards Trnka and himself. The stylistic variations in his animated films over time, in fact, demonstrate how Trnka has two major expressive sides: a spontaneous, rustic, peasant-like one, stemming from the popular puppet theater; and a more controlled and expressive one, that pushes his puppets towards the imitation of live cinema and the pursuit of technical perfection. According to Bendazzi (2015: 66), Trnka as a "peasant-poet [...] brought to cinema a deep love for nature and a lyric faith in tradition and their eternal spirit, which inspired his full-blooded sense of humour and his faith in life." Conversely, "the *refined, baroque* side of Trnka's work is the representation of a well-assimilated culture but is also the most open to criticism. Whenever the theme challenged his expressive skills, Trnka became more cerebral, even falling into a precious, but uninspired, style" (Bendazzi 2015: 66). The *stingers*, with their electronic artificiality and unabashed adherence to spectacular clichés, sound like a musical consequence of Trnka's second style, and especially so if one considers that artificial sounds dominate the most cerebral of Trnka's films, *The Hand*.

On a more positive note, because of their synchronic nature, the *stingers* might even be a transfigured *reincarnation* of the brash and provocative synchronic effects that sometimes were used in traditional puppet plays, such as the weird voices and calls that Skupa personally provided to his wooden protagonists (see Chapter 1). *A Midsummer Night's Dream* restored a direct link with the old style of Czech puppetry in many ways; its ending reinforces this impression, as the amateur actors perform. In that sequence, Trnka emphasizes that we are seeing actors on a stage; a wall is a puppet draped with a checkered cloth; the moon is the round face of another puppet dressed in black; a lion is a puppet with a hairy mask on. The costumes and props signal that the scene is to be perceived as theater enacted by puppets within a film, just like in the *Festival* segment from *The Czech Year*. The players are no more roughly sculpted or stringed, but they are all the same portrayed during a theatrical routine. It is actually relevant that no apparent difference exists between their movements and appearance during the act, and how they looked during the rest of the film. By this identity, and the lack of any cinematographic embellishment of the costumes and scenery (unlike *The Czech Year*, where the rough puppet were substituted for a fantasy sequence that showed how the characters should look in the mind of the spectators, creating a divide between theater and life), Trnka implicitly reaffirms that there is no difference between his puppet cinema and puppet theater; the former should be understood as a continuation of that popular stage culture and should keep using the stage language.

The finale also pays homage to Shakespeare's poetics. His actor-puppets, at the end of the film, disappear behind a red curtain; not just the amateur actors, but all the protagonists and sidekicks. "All

the world's a stage," said Jacques at the beginning of his monologue in Act II, Scene VII, Line 138 of Shakespeare's *As You Like
It*. In the case of Trnka's cinema, this is literally true: the world of
the puppets coincides with their stage and vice versa, as everything on screen is artificial and specifically built for the purpose
of animation. It does not live outside the film, except as a memory
or a dream. *A Midsummer's Night Dream*, in the end, does not
feel like "Shakespeare without Shakespeare"; the story and its animated treatment are imbued with the metatheatrical vision of the
English author, as seen through a multiform audiovisual entity
guided by the styles of Trnka and Trojan.

RUKA (THE HAND, 1965)

The years after 1959 were difficult ones, for both Trnka and Trojan.
The director returned to book illustration but grew progressively
wary of the control of the Czechoslovak socialist government over
any form of artistic expression. He developed a pessimistic state of
mind, paired with the self-conviction that nothing more was left
to be said with puppet cinema, save civic themes (Boillat 1974: 521;
Bendazzi 2015: 65). He returned to puppet film less than before,
and each time he shifted away from his lyrical side, conceding
more and more space to philosophical tales with social or political undertones, treated with unconventional visual solutions.
Such were the cases of the short films *Vášeň* (*The Passion*, 1961),
about a man who wastes his life to satisfy his passion for speed;
Kybernetická Babička (*The Cybernetic Grandma*, 1962; music by
Jan Novák), a science-fiction tale about the pitfalls of technology,
that shows the horrible fate of a little girl who, engrossed by scientific marvels, finds herself trapped in a futuristic apartment with
all the possible comforts, included a robotic grandma that replaces
her original one (who in the end comes to the rescue and comforts
her granddaughter with a traditional fairytale); and *Archanděl
Gabriel a paní Husa* (*The Archangel Gabriel and Mrs. Goose*, 1964;
music by Jan Novák), from Giovanni Boccaccio's *Decameron*, centered around a lecherous priest disguised as an archangel that, in a

Renaissance Venice, takes advantage of the beautiful and devoted Mrs. Goose, until he is ambushed by the lady's four brothers, kidnapped by a malicious old man and exhibited in public like a weird animal. Extreme stylization and grotesque excesses coexist in the designs of these films, that convey exacerbated feelings of contrast and uneasiness; the visual clashes are fostered also by variations in the animation technique; for example, in *The Archangel Gabriel and Mrs. Goose*, puppet scenes alternate with still drawings. In the same years, Trnka also contributed to short films by his collaborators; the civic and satiric theme of his interests was already present in the story idea he provided to *Bombomanie* (*Bombomania*, Břetislav Pojar, 1959), a hand-drawn short about a powerful explosive chemical discovered by a child, that in the hands of scientists and the military leads to the end of the world. Trnka's hand showed some of its lyrical side in some collaborations where he did not have to provide story content: the sceneries of the puppet film for children *Půlnoční příhoda* (*The Midnight Adventure*, Břetislav Pojar, 1960); and the character designs of the puppet TV shorts *Olověný vojáček* (*The Steadfast Tin Soldier*, Eduard Hofman, 1963), *Pastýřka a kominíček* (*The Shepherdess and the Chimney Sweep*, Eduard Hofman, 1963); and the hand-drawn *Blaho lásky* (*The Bliss of Love*, Jiří Brdečka, 1966).

In the same years, Trojan focused on music for the stage and the concert hall, developing a new interest in the accordion, an instrument frequently featured in the compositions in the final part of his career, often performed and advised by the renowned accordionist Milan Bláha. Trojan took a break from the stressful deadlines of film scoring; however, in 1962 he was ready to work again with Trnka, as he prepared to compose for *The Cybernetic Grandma*. Around that time, though, he suffered a severe heart attack, that he attributed to excessive tension and stress. Jan Novák took over his duties with Trnka.

In 1963, Trojan was declared partially disabled, with a medical recommendation to avoid any kind of work involving a deadline (Vičar 1989: 178). A new, prolonged creative crisis ensued. Even though Trojan still managed to create music until his death in 1983, he often did so by reworking his past works into new forms. In particular, the film scores for Trnka provided him with a rich source of inspiration: this resulted in a *genealogy* of concert and stage works based on the musical legacy of Trnka's films (see Appendix 2).

Nonetheless, Trojan and Trnka had a last chance to create a film together: *The Hand*, that was going to be Trnka's final work, except for the very short advertisement *Maxplatte, Maxplatten* (1965). *The Hand* is a satirical apologue on the deadly effects that the limitation of creativity can have on art and artists: an artisan tries to create a simple vase in his house, but a gigantic gloved hand repeatedly breaks in and molds the clay into a celebratory miniature version of itself, with a pointing second finger that implies a sententious authority. The artisan defends his vase and his independence in vain: the hand sieges him with assaults alternated with promises of high honors. At one point, the hand reveals the central metaphor of the film, becoming a puppeteer's hand that pulls string connected to the puppet's limbs. The artist is forced to sculpt effigies of the hand, but manages to escape. When he barricades himself in the house, a vase accidentally falls on his head and kills him, with tragic irony. The hand then tributes him a state funeral, making him appear as a worthy servant of the regime.

More than an ending point of the long cooperation between Trojan and Trnka, *The Hand* feels like a new start, from the audiovisual point of view; or, from another perspective, it could be a metaphoric fade-out, as the typical traits of that audiovisual language appear now fragmented and rarefied. There is no place for the generous amount of musical ideas that Trojan used to provide to Trnka's films in the past; a quick comparison between *The Hand* and *Grandpa Planted a Beet*, for example, would be telling in this respect. The scarcity of music in *The Hand* is consistent with the audiovisual treatment of the other Trnka shorts of the '60s: little or no dialogue, but sound effects and music in sync with the narrative rhythm. In *The Passion*, there is not even any original music at all, but only repertoire excerpts (including a few bars from Bach's *Toccata and Fugue* in D minor BWV 565). The synchronic arrangement of sound and image is not intended for Mickey-Mousing, but as an added emphasis: the synchronic sounds are often excessive, even oppressive in their overt allusive value, to create a sense of ridicule and grotesqueness. For example, the Bach insert in *The Passion* appears during the visual metaphor of the obsessed biker that feeds the fuel tank of his bike with anything he finds on his way, even works of art: the *Toccata and Fugue* provides a sense of impending doom (in fact, the man is going to have soon a serious accident) while illustrating the fact that the biker symbolically grabs the marble bust of a composer resting on a piano and throws it into the tank. However, the bust looks like Beethoven, not Bach, and the *Toccata and Fugue* is not for piano, but an organ piece; the wrong references are probably there as a shout out to the biker's ignorance and disregard for culture.

Such almost didactic audiovisual emphases are also part of *The Hand* and contribute to the *cerebral* style that Bendazzi and other scholars identified in the works of the late Trnka. The score and effects are closely intertwined and the timbres are mostly used alone, avoiding any orchestral combination; this contributes to a general sense of fragmentation, while reconnecting with the dramatic use of solo instruments that Trojan displayed in past film works, and especially in *Why UNESCO?* The only moments of *The Hand* that present a more comprehensive writing for ensemble are at the beginning: a couple of chamber pieces create a light, gallant mood around the artist and the titular hand, that at first seems a dignified and respectable apparition. The same happens when, later, the artist has a brief dream about a flower. Those are the only parts when Trojan's neoclassicism resurfaces, both in the melodic and harmonic language, as well as in the instrumental choices (pizzicato strings, flute, harpsichord). The rest of the score is a matter of single sounds, ostinatos, or dissonant passages, whose unsettling quality is often due to the use of artificial timbres. A hint of the past interdiegetic freedom of Trnka's *silent* films is the electronic ostinato on two notes (F and D) that mimics the sound of the lathe, when the artist puts it in motion. It works, because *The Hand* is a film without dialogue; it is not silent, as there are many sound effects, but the spectator is not led to expect overt and realistic sound synchronies. It is probably not a simple chance that this nod to the past audiovisual language of Trojan and Trnka appears together with an action that expresses the innocent creative joy of the character. In the rest of the film, in fact, the artists will be subject to the oppressive attentions of the hand. The audiovisual role of music becomes then that of a spatial atmosphere, thanks to the typical sound texture that Trojan used in such cases, as in *Old Czech Legends* or *A Midsummer Night's Dream*: a few, irregularly spaced notes with no clear pitch (here they are from low percussion instruments), enshrouded in layered reverberations that give out an impression of mysterious vastness. The percussion layer sometimes develops into a proper musical piece: brass instruments intervene, and a solemn but dissonant march elaborates on the meaning of the hand and its overbearing power. In *The Hand*, there is little of the graceful playfulness of past films like *The Emperor's Nightingale*, and nothing of the free folk references of *The Czech Year*. The place of sound in *The Hand* is that of an amplifier of what the images are already saying loudly: the meaning is inescapable, just like the tyranny of the hand.

Trnka died too early, at only 57 in 1969, because of a heart condition. He received a state funeral, exactly as had his puppet in *The Hand*. In his last year, his inspiration remained silent. He reportedly said, "My hand is intact, but my mind is empty" (Bendazzi 2015: 66).

The final balance of the collaboration between Trojan and Trnka, however, was by no means negative. Notwithstanding Trnka's short life, his film production was prolific; it was even more so when considering that the production time of an animated film is longer than that of an equivalent live-action one. The preference that Trnka accorded to Trojan's music created a prolonged testing ground for an audiovisual dialogue between two artistic personalities familiar with each other's style. This is quite a rare occurrence, both in animation and in cinema as a whole; director–composer relationships that go past the ten collaborations are a minority. The Trnka–Trojan filmography is unique in the specific field of puppet animation; no other cases have ever equaled their effort in quantity. In terms of quality, the films by Trnka and Trojan managed to bring together major cultural issues: they voiced the Czech national heritage by referring to historical folk themes but also went beyond them with creative elaborations, showing how vital the legacy of the stories and melodies they relied upon still were. The point of balance in this refined operation was probably the puppet itself, both as an ideal and as a material object. The puppet was a sign of the direct descendants of Trnka's cinema from the Bohemian puppet theater. It bore the torch of theater into film; however, its entrance into the new realm asked for aesthetic adaptations and adjustments. Trnka made it into a pure mime, believing that the *realistic* voice illusion of film dubbing would not work on it; he compensated for the lack of dialogue with enhancement of the expressive values of design, camerawork, lighting, and acting – and music, most importantly. The void left by the voice was filled to the brim, and beyond, with Trojan's scores; the *silent* choice of Trnka opened up a vast array of audiovisual possibilities, because of the fluid diegetic state of the puppet's world. At the same time, the slow movements of the puppet, so different from the more frenetic universe of hand-drawn pictures, permitted Trojan to develop ample pieces, tightly fitted to the needs of the film but also apt to be reworked into concert pieces. Even when the sensibilities of Trojan and Trnka shifted away in the final part of their collaboration, the puppet and its features still kept them together and offered more options to the new needs of the creators. Dialogue entered into this delicate balance, but the solution to the dilemma of the voice was found in *A Midsummer Night's Dream*, with its atmospheric use of spaces and leitmotifs. What Trnka and Trojan achieved seems today seldom relevant to the mainstream stop-motion film, which mostly uses audiovisual aesthetics close to that of 3D computer graphics films, which in turn continued the audiovisual practice of hand-drawn feature films. There are signs of it, however, in the claymation works from Aardman and in a huge number of smaller, independent short films that confront themselves with the enigmatic presence of the silent puppets, such as the works of the Quay Brothers or the Italian Stefano Bessoni. The legacy of Trnka and Trojan is more evident in the films by the Central European continuators of the Brothers in Tricks and the Loutkový film Praha, like Brdečka, Látal, Pojar, and, later, Jan Švankmajer. However, not one of them has ever replicated the biggest achievement of Trnka and Trojan: that is, the creation of five full-length puppet features. The results of this effort stand as a continuing testimony of the audiovisual potential that music can bestow upon a still-faced puppet, and the vastness of the audiovisual horizon that such small animate actors can expose to music.

Appendix 1

FILMOGRAPHY OF JIŘÍ TRNKA AND VÁCLAV TROJAN

The filmography lists all the films that involved Trnka and/or Trojan.

1936

- *Všudybylovo dobrodružství*

  The Adventures of a Ubiquitous Fellow

  Short film (puppets)

  Production: IRE-Film; Direction: Irena Dodalová, Karel Dodal; Story: Jan Černý; Screenplay: Irena Dodalová, Karel Dodal; Animation: Hermína Týrlová, Irena Dodalová, Karel Dodal; Artistic Collaboration: **Jiří Trnka**, Hermína Týrlová; Music: Jaroslav Ježek; black and white with toning, mono, 12'.

  Trnka adapted Skupa's puppet Hurvínek.

1942

- *Dlouhý, Široký a Bystrozraký*

  Tall, Broad, and Sharp-Eye-Sighted

  Unfinished film (live action)

Production: Nationalfilm; Direction: Miroslav Cikán; Based on: *Dlouhý, Široký a Bystrozraký*, by Karel Jaromír Erben; Screenplay: Miroslav Cikán, Jaroslav Mottl, Julius Kalaš; Cinematography: Ferdinand Pečenka; Set Designer: Jan Zázvorka; Costume Design: **Jiří Trnka**; Production Manager: Václav Dražil; Collaborator: Jaroslav Mach; Music: Julius Kalaš; Actors: Jindřich Plachta, František Černý. Ladislav Pešek, František Smolík, Karel Hradilák, Jiří Dohnal, Vladimír Salač, Anna Letenská, Zorka Janů.

1943

- *Práce a peníze*

  Work and Money

  Short documentary film (live action)

  Music: **Václav Trojan**

  Lost film.

1944

- *Černí myslivci*

  Gamekeepers in Black

  Unfinished film (live action)

  Production: Nationalfilm; Direction: Martin Frič; Based on: *Černí myslivci*, by Růžena Svobodová; Story: Karel Steklý; Screenplay: Bohumil Štěpánek, Martin Frič; Dialogues: Jindřich Elbl, Artuš Černík, Jan Drda, Karel Smrž; Cinematography: Václav Hanuš; Assistant Cinematographer: Alois Jiráček; Set Designer: Ferdinand Fiala; Costume Design: **Jiří Trnka**; Location Scouting: Oldřich Novotný, Karel Janout; Makeup: Miloslav Koubek, Antonín Mužík,

Jan Matoušek; Editing: Jan Kohout; Production Manager: Václav Dražil; Representative of the Production Manager: František Urbánek; Assistant Production Manager: Bohumil Svoboda; Professional Advisors: Miroslav Haller, Jiří Frejka, Ondřej Sekora; Collaborator: Antonín Frič, Joža Götzová, Čeněk Rendl, J. Fallada; Music: Josef Stelibský; Lyrics: K. M. Walló; Actors: Dana Medřická, Gustav Nezval, Jaroslav Průcha, L. H. Struna, Jindřich Plachta, Karel Dostal.

1945

- *Zasadil dědek řepu*

  Grandpa Planted a Beet (animated drawings)

  Short film

  Production: Československý filmový ústav, Bratři v triku; Director: **Jiří Trnka**; Based on: anonymous fairytale; Story: Jiří Trnka; Screenplay: Jiří Trnka, Eduard Hofman, Josef Vácha; Cinematography: Vladimír Novotný; Design: Jiří Trnka; Sound Design: Josef Zavadil; Production Manager: Jaroslav Jílovec; Animation: Stanislav Látal, Vladimír Novotný, Zdeněk Miler, Josef Kábrt, Karel Štrebl, Čeněk Duba, Břetislav Drašar, Václav Bedřich, Zdena Melichárková, Věra Satrapová, Karel Mann, Bohuslav Šrámek, Božena Kosařová, Jaroslav Možíš, Vojen Masník, Bořivoj Novák, Ivan Masník; Music: **Václav Trojan**; color, 1:1,37, mono, 10'.

1946

- *Zvířátka a petrovští*

  The Animals and the Bandits

  Short film (animated drawings)

Production: Československý filmový ústav, Bratři v triku; Director: **Jiří Trnka**; Assistant Director: Eduard Hofman; Based on: *Die Bremer Stadtmusikanten*, by the Brothers Grimm; Story: Jiří Trnka; Screenplay: Jiří Trnka, Eduard Hofman, Stanislav Látal, Karel Mann; Text of the narrator: František Hrubín; Design: Jiří Trnka; Editing: Helena Lebdušková; Art Direction: Jiří Trnka; Assistant to the Art Direction: Eduard Hofman; Sound Design: Emil Poledník; Head Animator: Boris Masník; Production Manager: Jaroslav Jílovec; Artistic Collaboration: Václav Bedřich, Čeněk Duba, Josef Kábrt, Bohuslav Šrámek, Karel Štrebl, Richard Bláha, Bořivoj Novák, Ivan Masník, Vojen Masník; Music: Oskar Nedbal, **Václav Trojan**; color, 1:1,37, mono, 9'.

- *Pérák a SS*

  The Springer and the SS

  Short film (animated drawings)

  Production: Československý filmový ústav, Bratři v triku; Director: **Jiří Trnka**; Story: Ota Šafránek; Screenplay: Jiří Trnka, Jiří Brdečka; Cinematography: Vladimír Novotný; Designer: Jiří Trnka; Art Direction: Jiří Trnka; Assistant to the Art Direction: Jiří Brdečka; Sound Design: Emanuel Formánek, AR Studio Lucerna, Praha; Animation: Stanislav Látal, Čeněk Duba, Josef Kábrt, Miloslav Krejčí, Karel Mann, Zdeněk Miler, Bohuslav Šrámek, Karel Štrebl; Production Manager: Jaroslav Jílovec; Artistic Collaboration: Zbyněk Bláha, Blahout, Rudolf Holan, Vojen Masník, Jaroslav Možíš, Bořivoj Novák, Music: Jan Rychlík; Orchestra: Filmový Symfonický Orchestr; Conductor: Milivoj Uzelac; black and white, 1:1,37, mono, 14'.

- *Dárek*

  The Gift

  Short film (animated drawings and live action)

  Production: Československý filmový ústav, Bratři v triku; Director (animated part): **Jiří Trnka**; Director (live-action part): Jiří Krejčík: Story: Jiří Brdečka, Jiří Trnka; Screenplay: Jiří Brdečka, Jiří Trnka, Eduard Hofman; Cinematography: Vladimír Novotný; Design: Jiří Trnka; Editing: Helena Lebdušková; Art Direction: Jiří Trnka; Sound Design: Josef Zavadil, AR Studio Lucerna, Praha; Production Manager: Jaroslav Jílovec; Artistic Collaboration: Václav Bedřich, Čeněk Duba, Josef Kábrt, Miloslav Krejčí, Stanislav Látal, Karel Mann, Ivan Masník, Vojen Masník, Zdeněk Miler, Bořivoj Novák, Vladimír Novotný, Josef Šiška, Bohuslav Šrámek, Karel Štrebl; Music: Jan Rychlík, color, 1:1,37, mono, 16'.

- *Vodník ve mlýně*

  The Vodník in the Mill

  Short film (animated drawings)

  Production: Československý státní film, Kreslený a loutkový film Praha; Director: Josef Vácha; Story: Richard Bláha; Screenplay: Josef Vácha; Art Direction: Karel Štrebl; Editing: Helena Lebdušková; Sound Design: Emanuel Formánek; Production Manager: Jaroslav Jílovec; Animation: Václav Bedřich, Čeněk Duba, Břetislav Dvořák, Josef Kábrt, Kosařová, Miloslav Krejčí, Stanislav Látal, Karel Mann, Müller, Břetislav Pojar, Bohuslav Šrámek, Ladislav Váňa, Vašek, Verdan; Artistic Collaboration: Janovský, Jaroslav Možíš, Josef Novák, Stroff; Professional Consultants: Prof. Vlastimil Rada, Jožka Šaršeová, Stanislav Neumann; Music: **Václav Trojan**; Orchestra: Filmový Symfonický Orchestr; Conductor: Otakar Pařík; color, 1:1,37, mono, 10'.

1947

- *Liška a džbán*

  The Fox and the Jug

  Short film (animated drawings)

  Production: Kreslený a loutkový film Praha; Directors: **Jiří Trnka**, Stanislav Látal;, Story: Josef Kábrt, Jan Karpaš; Screenplay: Jiří Trnka, Stanislav Látal; Design: Jiří Trnka; Art Direction: Jiří Trnka; Sound Design: Josef Zavadil, J. Kuncmann; Production Manager: Jaroslav Jílovec; Artistic Collaboration: Karel Štrebl, Václav Bedřich, Josef Kábrt, Zdeněk Miler, Jiří Vokoun, Břetislav Dvořák, Miloslav Krejčí, Karel Mann, Božena Možíšová, Verdan, Ladislav Váňa, Helena Lebdušková, Josef Novák, František Řehák; Music: Jan Kapr; Orchestra: Filmový Symfonický Orchestr; Conductor: Otakar Pařík; color, 1:1,37, mono, 9'.

- *Čapkovy povídky*

  Čapek's Tales

  Feature film (live action)

  Production: Československá výroba dlouhých filmů; Director: Martin Frič; Assistant Director: Vladimír Hladký; Based on: Karel Čapek's works; Story: Martin Frič, Jaroslav Žák; Screenplay: František Vlček; Dialogues: Věra Pečenková; Cinematography: Jan Roth; Assistant to cinematography: Rudolf Milič; Set Designer: Štěpán Kopecký; Assistant Set Designer: Vladimír Syrovátka; Costume Design: **Jiří Trnka**; Location Scouting: Prokop Pěkný; Costumes: Bohumil Sochor; Makeup: Gustav Hrdlička; Editing: Jan Kohout; Sound Design: Jan Paleček; Production Manager: Eduard Šimáček; Unit Production Manager: Bohuslav Kubásek; Professional Consultants: JUDr. Kitzner, Ing. Špátenko;

Music: František Škvor; Orchestra: Filmový Symfonický Orchestr; Choir: Dětský pěvecký sbor; Conductor: Otakar Pařík; Choirmaster: Jan Kühn; Actors: Jaroslav Marvan, Vladimír Hlavatý, Jaroslav Průcha, Vladimír Řepa, Gustav Hilmar, Felix le Breux, Ladislav Kulhánek, Lída Chválová, Jiřina Stránská, Blažena Slavíčková, Milada Smolíková; black and white, 1:1,37, mono, 106'.

- *Míša Kulička*

  Misha the Bear

  Short film (puppets)

  Production: Kreslený a loutkový film Praha; Directors: Karel Baroch, Eduard Hofman; Based on: *Míša Kulička v rodném lese*, by Josef Menzel; Story: Josef Menzel; Screenplay: Karel Baroch, Eduard Hofman; Cinematography: Vladimír Novotný, Jan Karpaš, Jan Novák; Art Direction: **Jiří Trnka**; Production Manager: Jaroslav Jílovec; Animation: Zdeněk Hrabě, Jan Karpaš, Břetislav Pojar, Bohuslav Šrámek, Arnošt Továrek; Music: František Škvor; color, 1:1,37, mono, 11'.

- *Špalíček*

  The Czech Year

  Feature film (puppets)

  Production: Kreslený a loutkový film Praha; Director, **Jiří Trnka**; Story: Jiří Trnka, Václav Trojan, Václav Renč; Screenplay, Jiří Trnka; Cinematography: Vladimír Novotný, Emanuel Franek; Art Director: Jiří Trnka; Set Designer: Jaroslav Zdrůbecký, František Braun, František Horník, V. Braun, Karel Sobotka; Editor: Jiří Trnka, Helena Lebdušková; Sound Design: Josef Zavadil; Production Manager: Jaroslav Jílovec; Unit Production Manager: Vladimír Janovský; Animation: Bohuslav Šrámek,

Břetislav Pojar, Jan Karpaš, Zdeněk Hrabě, Stanislav Látal, Arnošt Továrek; Artistic Collaboration: J. Reigrová, Václav Mervart, Jaroslav Zdrůbecký, Josef Zdrůbecký, Karel Sobotka, Milena Neubauerová; Consultants: Václav Trojan, Václav Renč; Music: **Václav Trojan**; Orchestra: Filmový Symfonický Orchestr; Choir: Dětský pěvecký sbor; Conductor: Otakar Pařík; Choirmaster: Jan Kühn; color, 1:1,37, mono, 76'.

1948

- *Císařův slavík*

  The Emperor's Nightingale

  Feature film (puppets)

  Production: Loutkový film Praha, Československý státní film Praha; Director: **Jiří Trnka**; Director (live-action): Miloš Makovec; Based on: *Nattergalen*, by Hans Christian Andersen; Screenplay: Jiří Trnka, Jiří Brdečka, Vítězslav Nezval; Shooting Script: Jiří Trnka; Cinematography: Ludvík Hájek (animation), Ferdinand Pečenka (live-action); Art Direction: Jiří Trnka; Editing: Jiří Trnka, Helena Lebdušková; Sound Design: Josef Zavadil; Production Manager: Bohumír Buriánek; Unit Production Manager: Vladimír Janovský; Artistic Collaboration: Milena Neubauerová, Karel Sobotka, František Braun, Erik Miloš Bülow, Josef Zdrůbecký, Jaroslav Zdrůbecký, Karel Mázel, Ludvík Hájek; Technical Collaboration: Emanuel Franek, Václav Mervart; Music: **Václav Trojan**; Solo violin: Ivan Kavaciuk; Orchestra: Filmový Symfonický Orchestr; Choir: Dětský pěvecký sbor; Conductor: Otakar Pařík; Choirmaster: Jan Kühn; Actors: Jaromír Sobota, Helena Patočková; color, 1:1,37, mono, 70'.

1949

- *Čertův mlýn*

  The Devil's Mill

  Short film (puppets)

  Production: Loutkový film Praha, Československý státní film Praha; Director: **Jiří Trnka**; Based on: anonymous fairy tale; Story: Jiří Trnka; Screenplay: Jiří Trnka; Cinematography: Emanuel Franek, Ludvík Hájek; Art Direction: Jiří Trnka; Editing: Helena Lebdušková; Sound Design: Emanuel Formánek, Josef Zavadil; Animation: Zdeněk Hrabě, Jan Karpaš, Stanislav Látal, Břetislav Pojar, Bohuslav Šrámek; Music: **Václav Trojan**; color, 1:1,37, mono, 21'.

- *Román s basou*

  The Tale of the Contrabass

  Short film (puppets)

  Production: Loutkový film Praha, Československý státní film Praha; Director: **Jiří Trnka**; Based on: "Romance with Double-Bass" by Anton Pavlovič Čechov; Story: Jiří Trnka; Screenplay: Jiří Trnka; Cinematography: Emanuel Franek, Ludvík Hájek; Art Direction: Jiří Trnka; Editing: Helena Lebdušková; Production Manager: Bohumír Buriánek; Unit Production Manager: Vladimír Janovský; Animation: Stanislav Látal, Jan Karpaš, Zdeněk Hrabě, Bohuslav Šrámek, Břetislav Pojar; Cooperation: František Braun, Karel Mázel, Václav Mervart, Milena Neubauerová, Karel Sobotka, Jaroslav Zdrůbecký; Music: **Václav Trojan**; Orchestra: Filmový Symfonický Orchestr; color, 1:1,37, mono, 21'.

- *Arie prerie*

  The Song of the Prairie

Short film (puppets)

Production: Loutkový film Praha, Československý státní film Praha; Director: **Jiří Trnka**; Story: Jiří Brdečka; Screenplay: Jiří Trnka; Cinematography: Emanuel Franek, Ludvík Hájek; Art Direction: Jiří Trnka; Editing: Helena Lebdušková; Production Manager: Bohumír Buriánek, Vladimír Janovský; Animation: Břetislav Pojar, Stanislav Látal, Jan Karpaš, Bohuslav Šrámek, Zdeněk Hrabě; Cooperation: František Braun, Karel Mázel, Václav Mervart, Milena Neubauerová, Josef Novák, Karel Sobotka, Aida Stockarová, Jaroslav Zdrůbecký; Music: Jan Rychlík; Orchestra: Filmový Symfonický Orchestr; Singers: Slávka Procházková, Oldřich Dědek; color, 1:1,37, mono, 21'.

1950

- *Bajaja*

Prince Bajaja

Feature film (puppets)

Production: Loutkový film Praha, Československý státní film Praha; Director: **Jiří Trnka**; Based on: *Princ Bajaja*, by Božena Němcová; Screenplay: Jiří Trnka, Karel Sobotka, Josef Novák, František Braun; Text of the commentary: Vítězslav Nezval; Cinematography: Ludvík Hájek, Emanuel Franek; Art Direction: Jiří Trnka; Editing: Helena Lebdušková; Sound Design: Josef Zavadil; Production Manager: Bohumír Buriánek; Unit Production Manager: Vladimír Janovský; Animation: Břetislav Pojar, Jan Karpaš, Bohuslav Šrámek, Zdeněk Hrabě, Stanislav Látal, František Braun; Cooperation: Karel Sobotka, Josef Novák, František Braun, Václav Mervart, Josef Zdrůbecký, Aida Stockarová, Karel Mázel, Jiří Vaněk, Milena Neubauerová; Music: **Václav Trojan**; Lyrics: Vítězslav Nezval; Orchestra: Filmový Symfonický Orchestr; Choir:

Dětský pěvecký sbor; Conductor: Otakar Pařík; Choirmaster: Jan Kühn; color, 1:1,37, mono, 71'.

- *Navrácený svět*

  The Returned World

  Short documentary film (live action)

  Music: **Václav Trojan**

  Lost film.

1951

- *Perníková chaloupka*

  The Gingerbread House

  Short film (puppets)

  Production: Loutkový film Praha, Československý státní film Praha; Director: Břetislav Pojar; Based on: anonymous fairy tale; Story: Břetislav Pojar; Screenplay: Břetislav Pojar; Cinematography: Ludvík Hájek; Art Director: **Jiří Trnka**; Editing: Helena Lebdušková, Milena Neubauerová; Sound Design: Emil Poledník; Animation: Jan Karpaš, Stanislav Látal, Zdeněk Hrabě; Music: Jiří Srnka; Orchestra: Filmový Symfonický Orchestr; Conductor: Otakar Pařík; color, 1:1,37, mono, 19'.

- *Císařův pekař – Pekařův císař*

  The Emperor's Baker – The Baker's Emperor/The Emperor and the Golem

  Feature film (live action)

  Production: Československý státní film; Director: Martin Frič; Assistant Director: Rudolf Jaroš; Story: Jan Werich,

Jiří Brdečka; Screenplay: Jan Werich, Jiří Brdečka, Martin Frič; Cinematography: Jan Stallich; Second Unit Cinematography: Bohumil Hába; Production Design: Jan Zázvorka; Art Director: Jaroslav Horejc; Costume Design: **Jiří Trnka**, Vladimír Synek; Makeup: Gustav Hrdlička; Editing: Jan Kohout; Sound Design: František Černý; Production Manager: Ladislav Terš, Rudolf Hájek; Unit Production Manager: Jaroslav Vlk; Music: Julius Kalaš; Songs: Zdeněk Petr; Lyrics: Jan Werich; Singer: Jan Werich; Choreographer: Luboš Ogoun, Jiřina Kottová; Orchestra: Filmový Symfonický Orchestr; Conductor: Milivoj Uzelac; Actors: Jan Werich, Marie Vášová, Nataša Gollová, Bohuš Záhorský, Jiří Plachý, Zdeněk Štěpánek, František Filipovský, František Černý, Václav Trégl, Vladimír Leraus, Miloš Nedbal, Bohuš Hradil; color, 1:1,37, mono, 155'.

The Czech version is in two parts; there is a one-part international version with a 112' runtime.

- *Veselý cirkus*

  The Merry Circus

  Short film (paper cut-outs)

  Production: Loutkový film Praha, Československý státní film Praha; Director: **Jiří Trnka**; Story: Jiří Trnka; Screenplay: Jiří Trnka; Shooting Script: Jiří Trnka; Cinematography: Emanuel Franek; Art Direction: Jiří Trnka, František Tichý, Kamil Lhoták, Zdeněk Seydl; Editing: Helena Lebdušková; Sound Design: Emanuel Formánek; Animation: Bohuslav Šrámek, Josef Kluge, Stanislav Látal; Music: **Václav Trojan**, Jan Rychlík; Orchestra: Filmový Symfonický Orchestr; Conductor: Otakar Pařík; color, 1:1,37, mono, 12'.

- *O zlaté rybce*

  The Golden Fish

  Short film (still images)

  Production: Kreslený film Praha, Československý státní film Praha; Director: **Jiří Trnka**; Based on: anonymous Russian fairy tale; Story: Jan Werich; Screenplay: Jiří Trnka; Text of the commentary: Jan Werich; Cinematography: Emanuel Franek, Josef Vágner; Art Direction: Jiří Trnka; Editing: Helena Lebdušková; Sound Design: Emanuel Formánek; Production Manager: Vojen Masník; Animation: Josef Kluge; Music: **Václav Trojan**; Voice Actor: Jan Werich.

1952

- *Staré pověsti české*

  Old Czech Legends

  Feature film (puppets)

  Production: Loutkový film Praha, Československý státní film Praha; Director: **Jiří Trnka**; Based on: *Staré pověsti české*, by Alois Jirásek; *Kronika Čechů/Chronica Boemorum* by Kosmas; Story: Jiří Trnka, Miloš V. Kratochvíl, Jiří Brdečka; Screenplay: Jiří Trnka, Jiří Brdečka; Text of the Commentary: Jiří Trnka; Shooting Script: Jiří Trnka; Cinematography: Ludvík Hájek, Emanuel Franek; Art Direction: Jiří Trnka; Editing: Helena Lebdušková; Sound Design: Emanuel Formánek, Emil Poledník, Josef Zavadil, Antonín Jedlička, Karel Mann; Productor: Vojen Masník, Vladimír Janovský, Jaroslav Možíš; Production Supervisor: Erna Kmínková; Animation: Břetislav Pojar, Bohuslav Šrámek, Zdeněk Hrabě, Stanislav Látal, Jan Karpaš, Josef Kluge, František Braun; Consultants: Dr. Rudolf Turek (archeology), Albert Pek (music history); Cooperation:

Karel Sobotka, František Braun, Josef Novák, Jiří Vaněk, Hynek Hlouch, Milena Nováková, Aida Stockarová, Václav Mervart, Jaroslav Zdrůbecký, Karel Mann; Music: **Václav Trojan**; Orchestra: Filmový Symfonický Orchestr; Choir: Český pěvecký sbor; Conductor: Otakar Pařík; Choirmaster: Jan Kühn; Voice Actors: Růžena Nasková, Václav Vydra sr., Karel Höger, Zdeněk Štěpánek, Eduard Kohout, Otomar Krejča; color, 1:1,37, mono, 85'.

1953

- *O skleničku víc*

  One Glass Too Many

  Short film (puppets)

  Production: Loutkový film Praha, Československý státní film Praha; Director: Břetislav Pojar; Story: Alois Macera; Screenplay: Jiří Brdečka, Břetislav Pojar; Cinematography: Emanuel Franek, Ludvík Hájek; Art Direction: **Jiří Trnka**; Editing: Helena Lebdušková; Sound Design: Emanuel Formánek, Josef Zavadil, Karel Mann, Antonín Jedlička; Producer: Jaroslav Možíš; Cooperation: Ministerstvo zdravotnictví ČSR, František Braun, Karel Sobotka, Josef Novák, Hynek Hlouch, Milena Nováková, Aida Stockarová, Marta Vlčková, Václav Mervart, Jaroslav Zdrůbecký, Brož; Animation: Zdeněk Hrabě, Jan Karpaš, Stanislav Látal, Josef Kluge; Music: Jan Rychlík; Lyrics: Jiří Brdečka; Singer: Setleři; Orchestra: Filmový Symfonický Orchestr; Conductor: Milivoj Uzelac; color, 1:1,37, mono, 18'.

- *Jak stařeček měnil až vyměnil*

  How the Old Man Traded It All Away

  Short film (still images)

Production: Loutkový film Praha, Československý státní film Praha; Director: **Jiří Trnka**; Based on: the fairy tale by František Bartoš; Screenplay: Jiří Trnka; Art Direction: Jiří Trnka; Editing: Helena Lebdušková; Sound Design: Emanuel Formánek; Production Manager: Jaroslav Možíš; Music: **Václav Trojan**; color, 1:1,37, mono, 9'.

1954

- *Byl jednou jeden král …*

  Once Upon a Time, There Was a King …

  Feature film (live action)

  Production: Studio uměleckého filmu; Director: Bořivoj Zeman; Assistant Director: Jiří Jungwirth, Pavel Kopta, Květa Ondráková; Based on: *Sůl nad zlato*, a fairy tale by Božena Němcová; Story: Jiří Brdečka, Oldřich Kautský, Jan Werich, Bořivoj Zeman; Screenplay: Jiří Brdečka, Jan Werich, Bořivoj Zeman; Cinematography: Jan Roth; Operator: Josef Pechar, Jiří Štaud; Production Designer: Jan Zázvorka; Art Direction: **Jiří Trnka**; Set Design: Vladimír Mácha; Costume Design: Bohumil Sochor; Makeup: Gustav Hrdlička; Editing: Josef Dobřichovský; Sound Design: Milan R. Novotný; Special Effects: Vladimír Novotný; Production Manager: Jaroslav Jílovec; Unit Production Manager: Vlastimil Maršálek; Consultant: Jan Port, PhD; Music: **Václav Trojan**; Lyrics: Jaroslav Seifert; Singers: Vlasta Burian, Vladimír Ráž, František Černý: Choreographer: Marie Anna Tymichová; Orchestra: Filmový Symfonický Orchestr; Conductor: Milivoj Uzelac; Actors: Jan Werich, Vlasta Burian, Irena Kačírková, Stella Májová, Milena Dvorská, František Černý, Lubomír Lipský, Miloš Kopecký, Miroslav Horníček. Terezie Brzková; color, 1:1,37, mono, 103'.

- *Jan Hus*

Jan Hus

Feature film (live action)

Production: Studio uměleckého filmu; Director: Otakar Vávra; Second Unit Director: Věra Ženíšková; Assistant Director: František Matoušek, Lenka Němečková; Based on: novels by Miloš V. Kratochvíl and Alois Jirásek; Story: Otakar Vávra, Miloš V. Kratochvíl; Screenplay: Miloš V. Kratochvíl, Otakar Vávra; Shooting Script: Otakar Vávra; Cinematography: Václav Hanuš; Operator: Josef Hanuš, Miloš Petrolín; Production Designer: Karel Škvor; Assistant Production Designer: Oldřich Okáč, Jaroslav Krška; Art Direction: **Jiří Trnka**, Vladimír Sychra, Jiří Josefík, František Pavlík, Jaroslav Alt, kolektiv malířů Akademie výtvarných umění; Set Design: Jan Janda; Costume Design: Jiří Trnka, Vladimír Synek, Fernand Vácha, J. M. Gottlieb; Costumes: Ladislav Tomek; Makeup: Otakar Košťál; Editing: Antonín Zelenka; Sound Design: František Černý; Special Effects: Chrudoš Uher, Milan Nejedlý, Vladimír Dvořák, Stanislav Šulc, Josef Bůžek, Jiří Šafář, Karel Císařovský, František Žemlička; Production Manager: František Milič; Unit Production Manager: Věra Třešková, Jaroslav Kučera; Consultants: Václav Mencl, Josef Macek, Jan Durdík, Eduard Wagner; Cooperation: Josef Pražák, Karel Ješátko, kolektiv krejčířské dílny na Barrandově; Music: Jiří Srnka; Singers: Zdeněk Štěpánek, Eduard Cupák, Josef Mixa, Antonín Šůra, Rudolf Hrušínský; Choreographer: Zora Šemberová, Laurette Hrdinová; Orchestra: Filmový Symfonický Orchestr; Choir: Český pěvecký sbor; Conductor: Milivoj Uzelac; Choirmaster: Jan Kühn; Actors:

Zdeněk Štěpánek, Karel Höger, Jan Pivec, Vlasta Matulová, Ladislav Pešek, Gustav Hilmar, Vítězslav Vejražka, Václav Voska, Eduard Kohout, Bedřich Karen, František Smolík, Otomar Krejča; color, 1:1,37, mono, 125'.

- *Osudy dobrého vojáka Švejka I.*

The Good Soldier Švejk – From Hatvan to Galicia/Fortunes of the Good Soldier Švejk in the World War

Short film (puppets)

Production: Loutkový film Praha; Director: **Jiří Trnka**; Based on: Jaroslav Hašek (novel), Josef Lada (illustrations); Screenplay: Jiří Trnka; Cinematography: Emanuel Franek; Art Direction: Josef Lada, Jiří Trnka; Editing: Helena Lebdušková, Jan Kohout; Sound Design: Emanuel Formánek; Producer: Jaroslav Možíš, Erna Kmínková, Věra Špeldová; Animation: Bohuslav Šrámek, Břetislav Pojar, Jan Karpaš; Cooperation: František Braun, Karel Sobotka, Václav Mervart, Milena Nováková, Marta Vlčková, Hynek Hlouch, Josef Novák, Jaroslav Zdrůbecký; Music: **Václav Trojan**; Orchestra: Filmový Symfonický Orchestr; Choir: Český pěvecký sbor; Conductor: Milivoj Uzelac; Voice Actor: Jan Werich; color, 1:1,37, mono, 23'.

- *Kuťásek a Kutilka jak ráno vstávali*

Kuťásek and Kutilka Woke Up in the Morning

Short film (live action and puppetry)

Production: Studio dětského filmu Praha; Director: **Jiří Trnka**; Story: Josef Pehr; Screenplay: Jiří Trnka; Cinematography: Vladimír Novotný; Operator: František Dojáček; Art Direction: Jiří Trnka; Editing: Helena Lebdušková; Sound Design: Emanuel Franek; Production Manager: Jaroslav Možíš; Cooperation: Kolektiv loutkového a dětského filmu; Music: **Václav Trojan**; Orchestra: Filmový Symfonický Orchestr; Conductor: Milivoj Uzelac; Actors: Josef Pehr, Luba Skořepová, Hana Vavrušková; color, 1:1,37, mono, 18'.

• *Dva mrazíci*

Two Ice Spirits

Short film (puppets and animated drawings)

Production: Loutkový film Praha; Director: **Jiří Trnka**; Assistant Director: Stanislav Látal; Based on: anonymous fairy tale; Story: Jiří Trnka; Screenplay: Jiří Trnka; Cinematography: Ludvík Hájek; Art Direction: Jiří Trnka; Editing: Helena Lebdušková; Sound Design: Emanuel Formánek; Production Manager: Jaroslav Možíš; Animation: Stanislav Látal, Břetislav Pojar, Zdeněk Hrabě, Jan Karpaš, Josef Kluge; Cooperation: František Braun, Karel Sobotka, Hynek Hlouch, Emanuel Franek, Václav Mervart, Josef Novák, Marta Vlčková, Milena Nováková, Aida Stockarová, Jaroslav Zdrůbecký; Music: Ilja Hurník; Performers: České noneto, Česká filharmonie; Conductors: Milan Munclinger (České noneto), Milan Munclinger (Česká filharmonie); Voice Actors: Vlasta Burian, Jan Werich; color, 1:1,37, mono, 12'.

1955

• *Spejbl na stopě*

Spejbl on the Trail

Short film (puppets)

Production: Loutkový film Praha; Director: Břetislav Pojar: Story: Vratislav Blažek, Břetislav Pojar; Screenplay: Vratislav Blažek, Břetislav Pojar; Cinematography: Emanuel Franek, Ludvík Hájek; Art Direction: **Jiří Trnka**; Editing: Marie Kopecká; Sound Design: Emanuel Formánek; Production Manager: Jaroslav Možíš, Erna Kmínková; Animation: Zdeněk Hrabě, Josef Kluge, Bohuslav Šrámek, Břetislav Pojar; Cooperation: Jiří Vaněk, Josef Novák, František

Braun, Marta Vlčková, Karel Sobotka, Václav Mervart, Hynek Hlouch, Jaroslav Zdrůbecký, Věra Špeldová; Music: Jan Rychlík; Singers: Oldřich Dědek, Miloš Kirschner; Orchestra: Filmový Symfonický Orchestr; Conductor: Milivoj Uzelac; Voice Actor: Josef Skupa; color, 1:1,37, mono, 22'.

- *Jan Žižka*

Jan Žižka

Feature film (live action)

Production: Studio uměleckého filmu; Director: Otakar Vávra; Second Unit Director: Věra Ženíšková; Assistant Director: František Matoušek, Lenka Němečková; Story: Otakar Vávra, Miloš V. Kratochvíl; Screenplay: Miloš V. Kratochvíl, Otakar Vávra; Shooting Script: Otakar Vávra; Cinematography: Václav Hanuš; Operator: Josef Hanuš, Miloš Petrolín; Production Designer: Karel Škvor; Assistant Production Designer: Oldřich Okáč; Art Direction: Jiří Josefík, František Pavlík, Jaroslav Alt; Set Design: Jan Janda, Václav Štědronský; Costume Design: **Jiří Trnka**, Vladimír Synek, Fernand Vácha, J. M. Gottlieb; Costumes: Ladislav Tomek; Makeup: Otakar Košťál; Editing: Antonín Zelenka; Sound Design: František Černý; Assistant Sound Designer: Václav Janoušek; Special Effects: Chrudoš Uher, Václav Hanuš, Milan Nejedlý, Vladimír Dvořák, Josef Bůžek, Karel Císařovský, František Žemlička; Production Manager: František Milič; Unit Production Manager: Věra Třešková, Jaroslav Kučera, Milan Kadlec; Consultants: Václav Mencl, Josef Macek, Jan Durdík, Eduard Wagner; Cooperation: Josef Pražák, František Tomeš, Karel Ješátko, vojska Československé lidové armády, Vojensko-historický ústav, jezdecké kluby Svazarmu, kolektiv krejčířské dílny na Barrandově; Music: Jiří Srnka; Singers: Alice Farkašová,

Vlastimil Brodský, Rudolf Hrušínský; Orchestra: Filmový Symfonický Orchestr; Choir: Pěvecký sbor Československého rozhlasu; Conductor: Milivoj Uzelac; Actors: Zdeněk Štěpánek, František Horák, Karel Höger, Jan Pivec, Vlasta Matulová, Ladislav Pešek, Gustav Hilmar, Vítězslav Vejražka, Václav Voska, Vítězslav Vejražka, Miloš Kopecký; color, 1:1,37, mono, 111'.

- *Kuťásek a Kutilka na pouti*

  Kuťásek and Kutilka at the Fair

  Short film (live action and puppetry)

  Production: Studio dětského filmu; Director: Stanislav Látal; Assistant Director: Josef Pehr; Story: Milan Pavlík; Story Adaptation: Stanislav Látal, Josef Pehr, Milan Pavlík; Art Direction: Divica Landrová, František Tichý; Cinematography: Ludvík Hájek; Assistant Cinematographer: Vl. Malík, V. Jireš; Editing: Josef Dobřichovský; Assistant Editor: L. Straňáková; Collaborators: František Braun, Hynek Hlouch, Václav Mervart, Jaroslav Zdrůbecký, Karel Sobotka, Věra Špeldová, Josef Novák, Marta Vlčková; Producer: Jaroslav Možíš, Erna Kmínková; Music: **Václav Trojan**; Orchestra: Nahrál Symfonický Orchestr; Conductor: František Belfín; Actors: Josef Pehr, František Tvrdek, Hana Vavrušková; Puppet Operators: Z. Hravě, Jan Karpaš, Stanislav Látal, Břetislav Pojar; color, 1:1,37, mono, 21'

- *Osudy dobrého vojáka Švejka II.*

  The Good Soldier Šveik – Šveik's Trouble on a Train/Fortunes of the Good Soldier Šveik in the World War

  Short film (puppets)

Production: Loutkový film Praha; Director: **Jiří Trnka**; Based on: Jaroslav Hašek (novel), Josef Lada (illustrations); Screenplay: Jiří Trnka; Cinematography: Emanuel Franek; Art Direction: Josef Lada, Jiří Trnka; Editing: Helena Lebdušková, Jan Kohout; Sound Design: Emanuel Formánek, Antonín Jedlička; Producer: Jaroslav Možíš, Erna Kmínková, Věra Špeldová; Animation: Bohuslav Šrámek, Břetislav Pojar, Jan Karpaš; Cooperation: František Braun, Karel Sobotka, Václav Mervart, Milena Nováková, Marta Vlčková, Hynek Hlouch, Josef Novák, Jaroslav Zdrůbecký; Music: **Václav Trojan**; Singer: Jan Werich; Orchestra: Filmový Symfonický Orchestr; Choir: Český pěvecký sbor; Conductor: Milivoj Uzelac; Voice Actor: Jan Werich; color, 1:1,37, mono, 21'.

- *Osudy dobrého vojáka Švejka III.*

  The Good Soldier Šveik – Šveik's Anabasis to Budejovice/ Fortunes of the Good Soldier Šveik in the World War

  Short film (puppets)

  Production: Loutkový film Praha; Director: **Jiří Trnka**; Assistant Director: Bohuslav Šrámek; Based on: Jaroslav Hašek (novel), Josef Lada (illustrations); Screenplay: Jiří Trnka; Cinematography: Emanuel Franek; Art Direction: Josef Lada, Jiří Trnka; Editing: Helena Lebdušková, Jan Kohout; Sound Design: Emanuel Formánek; Producer: Jaroslav Možíš, Erna Kmínková; Animation: Bohuslav Šrámek, Břetislav Pojar, Jan Karpaš, Břetislav Pojar, Zdeněk Hrabě; Cooperation: František Braun, Karel Sobotka, Václav Mervart, Vaněk, Marta Vlčková, Hynek Hlouch, Josef Novák, Věra Špeldová, Jaroslav Zdrůbecký; Music: **Václav Trojan**; Singers: Nelly Gaierová, Oldřich Dědek; Orchestra: Filmový Symfonický Orchestr; Choir: Český pěvecký sbor; Conductor: Milivoj Uzelac; Choirmaster: Jan Kühn; Voice Actor: Jan Werich; color, 1:1,37, mono, 30'.

- *Cirkus Hurvínek*

  Hurvínek's Circus

  Short film (puppets)

  Production: Loutkový film Praha, Československý státní film Praha; Director: **Jiří Trnka**; Assistant Director: Stanislav Látal; Story: Vratislav Blažek; Screenplay: Vratislav Blažek, Jiří Trnka; Shooting Script: Jiří Trnka; Cinematography: Ludvík Hájek; Art Direction: Jiří Trnka; Editing: Helena Lebdušková, Věra Špeldová; Sound Design: Emanuel Formánek; Production Manager: Jaroslav Možíš, Erna Kmínková; Animation: Stanislav Látal, Zdeněk Hrabě, Jan Karpaš, Josef Kluge; Cooperation: František Braun, Hynek Hlouch, Milena Nováková, Josef Novák, Václav Mervart, Karel Sobotka, Jiří Vaněk, Marta Vlčková, Jaroslav Zdrůbecký; Music: Jan Rychlík; Choir: Dětský pěvecký sbor; Conductor: Jaromír Nohejl; Choirmaster: Jan Kühn; Voice Actor: Josef Skupa; color, 1:1,37, mono, 25'.

1956

- *Proti všem*

  Against All

  Feature film (live action)

  Production: Filmové studio Barrandov; Director: Otakar Vávra; Second Unit Director: Věra Ženíšková; Assistant Director: František Matoušek; Based on: the novel by Alois Jirásek; Script Supervisor: Lenka Němečková; Screenplay: Miloš V. Kratochvíl, Otakar Vávra; Cinematography: Václav Hanuš; Second Unit Cinematography: Josef Pechar; Operator: Josef Hanuš, Miloš Petrolín; Production Design: Karel Škvor; Assistant Production Designer: Oldřich Okáč; Art Director: František Pavlík; Set Design: Václav Štědronský;

Costume Design: **Jiří Trnka**, Vladimír Synek; Costumes: Ladislav Tomek; Makeup: Otakar Košťál; Editing: Antonín Zelenka; Sound Design: František Černý; Assistant Sound Designer: Václav Janoušek; Special Effects: Chrudoš Uher, Václav Hanuš, Milan Nejedlý, Vladimír Dvořák, Josef Bůžek, Karel Císařovský, František Žemlička; Production Manager: František Milič; Unit Production Manager: Věra Třešková, Jaroslav Kučera, Milan Kadlec; Consultants: Václav Mencl, Josef Macek, Jan Durdík, Eduard Wagner; Cooperation: Josef Pražák, Karel Ješátko, vojska Československé lidové armády, Vojensko-historický ústav, jezdecké kluby Svazarmu, kolektiv krejčířské dílny na Barrandově; Music: Jiří Srnka; Choreographer: Jiří Němeček; Orchestra: Filmový Symfonický Orchestr; Choir: Pěvecký sbor Armádního uměleckého souboru Víta Nejedlého; Conductor: František Belfín; Actors: Zdeněk Štěpánek, Jan Pivec, Vlasta Matulová, Gustav Hilmar, Václav Voska, Bedřich Karen, Miroslav Doležal, Jana Rybářová; color, 1:1,37, mono, 109'.

1957

- *Paraplíčko*

  The Little Umbrella

  Short film (puppets)

  Production: Loutkový film Praha; Director: Břetislav Pojar; Story: Vratislav Blažek, Břetislav Pojar; Screenplay: Břetislav Pojar; Cinematography: Ludvík Hájek, Emanuel Franek; Art Direction: **Jiří Trnka**, Zdeněk Seydl, František Braun; Editing: Marie Kopecká; Sound Design: Emanuel Formánek; Production Manager: Jaroslav Možíš; Animation: Bohuslav Šrámek, Josef Kluge, Stanislav Látal, Břetislav Pojar; Cooperation: Václav Mervart, Hynek Hlouch, Marta Vlčková, Josef Novák, Jaroslav Zdrůbecký,

Karel Sobotka, Jiří Vaněk; Music: Miloš Vacek; color, 1:1,37, mono, 17'.

Trnka made the puppet of the goblin.

1958

- *Proč UNESCO*

  Why UNESCO?

  Short film (animated drawings)

  Production: Studio kresleného a loutkového filmu Praha, Bratři v triku; Director: **Jiří Trnka**; Story: Adolf Hoffmeister, Jiří Trnka; Screenplay: Jiří Trnka, Jiří Brdečka, Adolf Hoffmeister: Text of the Commentary: Jiří Trnka, Jiří Brdečka; Cinematography: Zdena Hajdová, Ivan Masník; Art Direction: Jiří Trnka; Editing: Zdena Navrátilová; Sound Design: František Černý; Production Manager: Vladislav Hofman; Animation: František Vystrčil; Music: **Václav Trojan**; color, 1:1,37, mono, 11'.

1959

- *Bombomanie*

  Bombomania

  Short film (animated drawings)

  Production: Krátký film Praha, Studio Bratři v triku, Studio kresleného filmu Praha; Director: Břetislav Pojar; Assistant Director: Jaroslav Doubrava; Story: Břetislav Pojar; Screenplay: Jiří Brdečka, Břetislav Pojar; Cinematography: Ivan Masník; Art Direction: **Jiří Trnka**; Editing: Jana Šebestíková; Sound Design: Josef Vlček, Antonín Jedlička; Production Manager: Jiří Šebestík; Animation: Karel Štrebl,

František Vystrčil, Ladislav Čapek, Jiří Vokoun, Břetislav Dvořák, Věra Marešová, Antonín Bureš, Š. Zavřel, Krista Vodičková, O. Vlásková, V. Janoušková; Cooperation: Bohumil Šiška, Z. Najmanová, I. Skála, H. Linhartová, M. Pechanová, J. Pošva; Music: Jan Rychlík; Orchestra: Filmový Symfonický Orchestr; Conductor: Štěpán Koníček; color, 1:1,37, mono, 11'.

- *Sen noci svatojanské*

  A Midsummer Night's Dream

  Feature film (puppets)

  Production: Studio kresleného a loutkového filmu Praha; Director: **Jiří Trnka**; Based on: *A Midsummer Night's Dream*, by William Shakespeare; Screenplay: Jiří Trnka, Jiří Brdečka; Text of the Commentary: Josef Kainar; Cinematography: Jiří Vojta; Art Direction: Jiří Trnka, Jaroslav Kulhánek; Editing: Hana Walachová; Sound Design: Emanuel Formánek, Josef Vlček, Emil Poledník, Jiří Horčička; Producer: Jaroslav Možíš, Erna Kmínková; Production Manager: Jiří Vaněk; Animation: Stanislav Látal, Bohuslav Šrámek, Jan Karpaš, Břetislav Pojar, Jan Adam, Vlasta Jurajdová; Artistic Collaboration: František Braun, Josef Novák, Karel Sobotka, Václav Mervart, Josef Zdrůbecký, Hynek Hlouch, Marta Vlčková, Věra Matějů, Garik Seko; Consultant: Břetislav Hodek; Cooperation: E. Tchýn, Jindřich Hrdina, Gustav Bezděkovský; Music: **Václav Trojan**; Choreographer: Ladislav Fialka, Ludmila Kovářová; Orchestra: Česká filharmonie; Choir: Kühnův dětský sbor; Conductor: Karel Ančerl; Choirmaster: Markéta Kühnová; Voice Actor: Rudolf Pellar; color, 1:2,35, stereo, 73'.

- *Skutečnost Noci svatojánské*

  A Midsummer's Night Reality

Short documentary film (live action)

Production: Krátký film Praha, Dokumentární film Praha; Director: Václav Táborský; Story: Václav Táborský; Screenplay: Jiří Blažek, Václav Táborský; Text of the Commentary: Václav Táborský; Cinematography: Jaroslav Šulc; Editing: Vlasta Styblíková; Sound Design: Miroslav Letenský; Production Manager: Josef Pivoňka; Music: **Václav Trojan**; color, 1:1,37, mono, 6'.

1960

- *Půlnoční příhoda*

  The Midnight Adventure

  Short film (puppets)

  Production: Studio kresleného a loutkového filmu Praha, Krátký film Praha; Director: Břetislav Pojar; Screenplay: Břetislav Pojar; Script Editor: Josef Menzel; Cinematography: Jiří Vojta, Jindřich Hrdina, Gustav Bezděkovský; Art Direction: **Jiří Trnka**; Editing: Hana Walachová; Sound Design: Emanuel Formánek; Production Manager: Jaroslav Možíš, Jiří Vaněk; Unit Production Manager: Erna Kmínková; Animation: Bohuslav Šrámek, Vlasta Pospíšilová, Stanislav Látal; Cooperation: Karel Sobotka, František Braun, Josef Novák, Pavel Šimák, Václav Mervart, Jaroslav Zdrůbecký, Marta Vlčková, Věra Matějů; Music: Wiliam Bukový; Orchestra: Filmový Symfonický Orchestr; Conductor: František Belfín; color, 1:1,37, mono, 14'.

- *Srpnová neděle*

  A Sunday in August

  Feature film (live action)

Production: Filmové studio Barrandov; Director: Otakar Vávra; Second Unit Director: Václav Sklenář; Assistant Director: Jan Schmidt; Based on: the play by František Hrubín; Screenplay: Otakar Vávra, Otomar Krejča, František Hrubín; Shooting Script: Otakar Vávra; Cinematography: Jaroslav Tuzar; Operator: Jiří Vojta, Ivan Šlapeta; Production Designer: Jaroslav Krška; Art Director: Josef Svoboda; Set Designer: Eva Slívová; Costume Designer: Jindřiška Hirschová; Costumes: Aša Teršová, Věra Hromádková; Makeup: Otakar Košťál, Václav Volk, Marie Zedníková, Alena Hejdánková; Editing: Antonín Zelenka; Sound Design: Miloslav Hůrka; Production Manager: Ladislav Terš; Unit Production Manager: Jaroslav Merunka, Ludmila Venclíková; Music: **Václav Trojan**; Songs: Václav Trojan, Johan B. Blobner; Lyrics: František Hrubín; Singer: Jiřina Šejbalová; Orchestra: Filmový Symfonický Orchestr; Conductor: František Belfín; Actors: Vlasta Fabianová, Karel Höger. Bohuš Záhorský. Jiřina Šejbalová. Miloš Nedbal, Miriam Hynková, Luděk Munzar, Otomar Krejča, color, 1:2,35, mono, 83'.

1961

• *Vášeň*

The Passion

Short film (puppets)

Production: Studio kresleného a loutkového filmu Praha, Krátký film Praha; Director: **Jiří Trnka**; Story: Jiří Trnka; Screenplay: Jiří Trnka; Script Editor: Josef Menzel; Cinematography: Jiří Šafář; Art Direction: Jiří Trnka; Editing: Hana Walachová; Sound Design: Emanuel Formánek; Production Manager: Jaroslav Možíš, Jiří Vaněk; Unit Production Manager: Erna Kmínková; Animation:

Bohuslav Šrámek, Jan Adam, Zdeněk Šob, Jan Karpaš; Cooperation: Gustav Bezděkovský, František Braun, Hynek Hloch, Věra Matějů, Václav Mervart, Josef Novák, Karel Sobotka, Pavel Šimák, Marta Vlčková, Josef Zdrůbecký; Music: archival music; color, 1:1,37, mono, 9'.

1962

- *Kybernetická babička*

  The Cybernetic Grandma

  Short film (puppets)

  Production: Studio kresleného a loutkového filmu Praha, Krátký film Praha; Director: **Jiří Trnka**; Story: Ivan Klíma; Screenplay: Jiří Trnka; Cinematography: Jiří Šafář; Operator: Ivan Renč; Art Direction: Jiří Trnka; Editing: Hana Walachová; Sound Design: Emanuel Formánek; Production Manager: Jaroslav Možíš, Jiří Vaněk; Unit Production Manager: Erna Kmínková; Animation: Stanislav Látal, Jan Adam, Vlasta Pospíšilová, Zdeněk Šob; Cooperation: Gustav Bezděkovský, František Braun, Hynek Hlouch, Václav Mervart, Josef Novák, Karel Sobotka, Pavel Šimák, Marta Vlčková, Jaroslav Zdrůbecký; Music: Jan Novák; Voice Actors: Otylie Beníšková. Jana Werichová; color, 1:1,37, mono, 30'.

1963

- *Olověný vojáček*

  The Steadfast Tin Soldier

  TV short film (puppets)

  Director: Eduard Hofman

  Trnka was the art director.

- *Pastýřka a kominíček*

  The Shepherdess and the Chimney Sweep

  TV short film (puppets)

  Director: Eduard Hofman

  Trnka was the art director.

1964

- *Limonádový Joe aneb Koňská opera*

  Lemonade Joe

  Feature film (live action)

  Production: Filmové studio Barrandov; Director: Oldřich Lipský; Second Unit Director: Tomáš Svoboda; Assistant Director: Marie Hejzlarová, Miloš Kohout; Based on: the novel and the play by Jiří Brdečka; Screenplay: Jiří Brdečka, Oldřich Lipský; Shooting Script: Jiří Brdečka, Oldřich Lipský; Cinematography: Vladimír Novotný; Second Unit Cinematography: Miloš Petrolín; Operator: Emil Hora, Jiří Knotek; Production Designer: Karel Škvor; Art Director: **Jiří Trnka**, Břetislav Pojar (for the animated insert, from *The Song of the Prairie*); Set Designer: Ladislav Krbec, Miloš Osvald, Jiří Rulík; Costume Designer: Jiří Brdečka, Fernand Vácha; Costumes: František Zapletal, Nita Romanečová, Eva Lackingerová; Makeup: Otakar Košťál, František Klema, Marie Zedníková, Miroslava Miškovská; Editing: Miroslav Hájek; Sound Design: Josef Vlček, Bohumír Brunclík, Antonín Jedlička; Special Effects: Vladimír Novotný, Ludvík Malý; Title Design: Vladimír Dvořák, Vlasta Jelínková; Production Manager: Jaroslav Jílovec; Unit Production Manager: Jaroslav Koucký, Miloš Stejskal, Renée Lavecká; Cooperation: Jiří Brdečka, Jana Fassatiová, Jitka

Šulcová, Jan Kňákal, Jindřich Aleš, Karel Ješátko, Státní hřebčín v Kladrubech; Music: Jan Rychlík, Vlastimil Hála; Lyrics: Jiří Brdečka, Pavel Kopta, Vratislav Blažek; Singers: Olga Schoberová, Jarmila Veselá, Waldemar Matuška, Květa Fialová, Yvetta Simonová, Miloš Kopecký, Karel Fiala, Karel Gott; Choreographer: Josef Koníček; Orchestra: Orchestr Karla Vlacha, Filmový Symfonický Orchestr; Conductor: Štěpán Koníček (Filmový Symfonický Orchestr), Karel Vlach (Orchestr Karla Vlacha); Actors: Karel Fiala, Miloš Kopecký, Rudolf Deyl jr., Květa Fialová, Olga Schoberová, Bohuš Záhorský, Josef Hlinomaz, Karel Effa; black and white (tinted), 1:2,35, mono, 98'.

- *Archanděl Gabriel a paní Husa*

  The Archangel Gabriel and Mrs. Goose

  Short film (puppets)

  Production: Studio kresleného a loutkového filmu Praha, Krátký film Praha; Director: **Jiří Trnka**; Second Unit Director: Jaroslav Možíš; Based on: *Decameron*, by Giovanni Boccaccio; Story: Jiří Trnka; Screenplay: Jiří Trnka; Script Editor: Jan Poš; Cinematography: Jiří Šafář; Art Direction: Jiří Trnka; Editing: Hana Walachová; Sound Design: Emanuel Formánek, František Černý; Production Manager: Erna Kmínková, Jiří Vaněk; Animation: Stanislav Látal, Vlasta Pospíšilová, Bohuslav Šrámek; Cooperation: Marta Vlčková, Josef Novák, František Braun, Václav Mervart, Karel Sobotka, Jaroslav Zdrůbecký, Pavel Šimák, Hynek Hlouch, Helena Veselá, Gustav Bezděkovský; Music: Jan Novák; color, 1:1,37, mono, 29'.

- *Neposlušná písmenka*

  The Disobedient Letters

  Short film (paper cut-outs)

Production: Studio kresleného a loutkového filmu, Krátký film Praha; Director: Bohuslav Šrámek; Story: Bohuslav Šrámek; Screenplay: Bohuslav Šrámek; Script Editor: Jan Poš; Cinematography: Jiří Šafář; Editing: Hana Walachová; Art Direction: Oldřich Jelínek; Animation: Bohuslav Šrámek; Music: **Václav Trojan** adapted and orchestrated music by Hermann Dostal, Archibald Joyce, Richard Eilenberg, Gioachino Rossini and himself; color, 1:1,37, mono, 12'.

1965

- *Ruka*

  The Hand

  Short film (puppets)

  Production: Studio kresleného a loutkového filmu, Krátký film Praha; Director: **Jiří Trnka**; Story: Jiří Trnka; Screenplay: Jiří Trnka; Script Editor: Jan Poš; Cinematography: Jiří Šafář; Art Direction: Jiří Trnka; Editing: Hana Walachová; Sound Design: Miloš Alster, Emil Poledník; Production Manager: Jiří Vaněk; Animation: Bohuslav Šrámek, Jan Adam; Cooperation: kolektiv loutkového filmu; Music: **Václav Trojan**; Actor (The Hand): Ladislav Fialka; color, 1:1,37, mono, 18'.

- *Maxplatte, Maxplatten*

  Maxplatte, Maxplatten

  Advertisement (puppets)

  Director: **Jiří Trnka**; Screenplay: Jiří Trnka; Art Direction: Jiří Trnka; Cinematography: Jiří Šafář; Animation: Bohuslav Šrámek, Vlasta Pospíšilová; Music: archival music; color, 1:1,37, mono, 2'.

1966

- *Blaho lásky*

  The Bliss of Love

  Short film (animated drawings)

  Production: Studio kresleného a loutkového filmu Praha, Krátký film Praha; Director: Jiří Brdečka; Story: Jiří Brdečka; Screenplay: Jiří Brdečka; Script Editor: Jindřich Vodička, Jan Poš; Cinematography: Ivan Masník; Art Direction: **Jiří Trnka**; Editing: Květa Mašková; Sound Design: Josef Vlček, Adolf Řípa; Production Manager: Jiří Šebestík, Václav Strnad; Animation: Božena Možíšová; Music: Jan Novák; archival music by Jean Paul Egide Martini; Singers: Helena Blehárová, Waldemar Matuška; color, 1:1,37, mono, 8'.

- *Poslední růže od Casanovy*

  The Last Rose from Casanova

  Feature film (live action)

  Production: Filmové studio Barrandov; Director: Václav Krška; Second Unit Director: Vladimír Zelenka; Assistant Director: Boca Abrhámová, Dagmar Zelenková; Story: František Daniel, František A. Dvořák; Screnplay: František Daniel, František A. Dvořák; Cinematography: Václav Hanuš; Second Unit Cinematography: Jaroslav Kupšík; Operator: Antonín Vojáček; Production Designer: Boris Moravec; Set Designer: Karel Kočí, Bohuslav Varhaník, Jaroslava Vilímková; Costume Designer: Jan Skalický; Costumes: Emílie Kůtová, Nita Romanečová; Makeup: Anežka Kunová, Marie Džbánková, Jiří Budín, Alena Čutková; Editing: Jan Kohout; Sound Design: Jaromír Svoboda; Production Manager: Gustav Rohan; Unit

Production Manager: Jan Syrový, Dana Dudová, Zora Rumlová; Cooperation: Luďka Žáková, Jarmila Müllerová, Jiří Kotlář; Music: **Václav Trojan**; Singer: Felix le Breux; Choreographer: Vlastimil Jílek; Dancers: Balet Národního divadla Praha; Performers: Filmový Symfonický Orchestr, Dvořákovo kvarteto; Conductor: František Belfín; Actors: Felix le Breux, Bohuš Záhorský, Vladimír Brabec, Milena Dvorská, Otto Šimánek, Libuše Havelková, Valja Petrová, Zuzana Šavrdová; black and white, 1:2,35, mono, 93'.

1967

- *Kolotoč*

  Merry-Go-Round

  Feature TV opera film (live action)

  Director: Václav Hudeček; Screenplay: Václav Hudeček; Cinematography: Jiri Volbracht;

  Music: **Václav Trojan**, from his own 1941 opera; Actors: Čestmír Řanda sr.., Vlastimil Hašek, Rudolf Pellar, Růžena Lysenková, Eva Víšková, Veronika Renčová, Dalibor Jedlička; black and white, 1:1,37, mono, 50'.

1968

- *Záhořanský hon*

  The Hunt of Zahořany

  Feature TV film (live action)

  Production: Ceskoslovenská televize Praha; Director: Bohumil Sobotka; Based on: the novel by Alois Jirásek; Screenplay: František Daniel, František A. Dvorák; Cinematography: Jaroslav Tuzar; Editing: Dana Lukesová;

Music: **Václav Trojan**; Actors: Jirí Nemecek, Jirí Bednár, Jan Preucil, Jaroslav Satoranský, Bohus Záhorský, Svatopluk Benes, Jan Skopecek; black and white, 1:1,37, mono, 87'.

1970

- *Václav Trojan: Slavík*

  Václav Trojan: The Nightingale

  Medium-length TV ballet film (live action)

  Production: Ceskoslovenská televize Praha; Director: Vlasta Janečková; Based on: *Nattergalen*, by Hans Christian Andersen; Screenplay: Vlasta Janečková; Cinematography: Milan Dostál; Editing: Olga Werzonová; Music: **Václav Trojan**, from the 1948 film by Trnka; Actors: Ladislav Pešek, Svatopluk Beneš, Milan Neděla, Eva Hrušková, František Holar, Karel Čížek, Jiřina Knížková, Angelo Michajlov, Pavel Ždichynec ; black and white, 1:1,37, mono, 41'.

1975

- *Zlatá brána*

  The Golden Gate

  Feature ballet TV film (live action)

  Production: Ceskoslovenská televize Praha; Director: Ivan Kotrč, Marcel Dekanovský; Assistant Director: Tamara Čopová; Story: Karel Plicka; Screenplay: Ivan Kotrč, Alica Takáčová; Cinematography: Ilja Bojanovský, Jozef Hardoš; Music: **Václav Trojan**, from his own 1974 ballet; Performers: Československého státního souboru písní a tanců; color, 1:1,37, mono, 92'.

1985

- *Sen noci ...*

The Night's Dream ...

Feature ballet film (live action)

Production: Filmové studio Barrandov; Director: Vladimír Sís; Second Unit Director: Milan Klacek; Assistant Director: Kryštof Hanzlík, Zdenka Barochová, Alena Sísová; Based on: *A Midsummer Night's Dream*, by William Shakespeare; ballet libretto by Alena Hoblová and Václav Trojan; Screenplay: Vladimír Sís; Shooting Script: Vladimír Sís; Script Editor: Alexander Lukeš; Cinematography: Jan Kališ; Second Unit Cinematography: Rudolf Holan, Jiří Ondráček, Martin Kubala; Operator: Tomáš Hampl, Stanislav Šťastný; Production Design: Jan Zázvorka, Karel Vacek; Art Direction: Jan Souček; Set Design: Miroslav Fára, Jaroslav Česal, Vladimír Ježek, Karel Kočí, Petr Průša; Costume Design: Alena Hoblová; Costumes: Ludmila Muchová, Stanislav Janeček, Petra Barochová, Zuzana Bursíková, Martina Zikmundová, Iveta Rosenbergerová; Makeup: Rudolf Kurel, Jana Dolejší, J. Kurelová, Libuše Beranová, J. Guttová, Jaroslav Šámal, Petr Fadrhons; Editing: Jaromír Janáček; Sound Design: Ivo Špalj, Jiří Zobač; Special Effects: Jiří Šimunek, Boris Masník, Ludvík Malý, Milan Nejedlý, Michael Poledník, Miroslav Šnábl; Production Manager: Jaromír Lukáš; Unit Production Manager: Milana Melcerová, Dagmar Pitráková, Jiří Synek, Martina Petrů, Ondřej Sláma; Cooperation: Yvona Limberská, Anna Mejtská, Eliška Willigová, Karel Vacek, Štěpán Exner, Miloš Preclík, Helena Friedlová, Jiří Kučera; Music: **Václav Trojan**; Choreographer: Luboš Ogoun; Orchestra: Filmový

Symfonický Orchestr; Conductor: Jan Štych; Performers: Jiří Kyselák, Dagmar Maštalířová, Lubomír Večeřa, Soňa Zejdová, Zdeněk Kárný, Eva Trnková, Zdeněk Hanzlovský, Jarmila Bařinková, Antonín Michna, Milan Potůček; color, 1:1,37, mono, 72'.

Appendix 2

COMPOSITIONS BY VÁCLAV TROJAN INSPIRED BY JIŘÍ TRNKA'S FILMS

From *Špaliček* (*The Czech Year,* 1947)

1951

- *Betlém*

  Bethlehem

  Suite of Christmas carols for soloists and children's choir accompanied by flute, oboe, clarinet, bass clarinet, harp, and organ.

1953

- *Dupák*

  Dupák

  For orchestra.

  Dance from the film score.

1953, 1977, 1981

- *Špaliček*

  The Czech Year

Suite for children's choir and orchestra.

Three suites based on different selections from the film score.

1967

- *Vrták*

  Vrták

  For orchestra.

  Dance from the film score. The score is lost.

1968

- *Špaliček*

  The Czech Year

  Suite for children's choir and piano (and solo instruments *ad libitum*).

  This suite is relatively different from the film music from the orchestral versions.

From *Císařův slavík* (*The Emperor's Nightingale*, 1949)
1949

- *Slavíkův koncert*

  Concert of the Nightingale

  For orchestra.

- *Žabák*

  The Frog

  For orchestra.

1950

- *Císařův slavík*

  The Emperor's Nightingale

  Suite for orchestra.

1953

- *Slavíkův koncert*

  Concert of the Nightingale

  For violin and piano.

  Violin part revised by Ivan Kawaciuk.

1964

- *Císařův slavík*

  The Emperor's Nightingale

  Suite for violin, guitar, and accordion.

1970

- *Slavík a smrt*

  The Nightingale and the Death

  For violin and piano.

  The violin part was revised by Ladislav Štibor.

1975

- *Slavík a smrt*

  The Nightingale and the Death

  For string quartet.

1982

- *Císařův slavík*

  The Emperor's Nightingale

  Suite for accordion and electrophonic accordion.

From *Čertův mlýn* (*The Devil's Mill*, 1949)
1950

- *Čertův mlýn*

  The Devil's Mill

  Suite for orchestra.

From *Zazděná* (*Walled In*, 1949)
1949

- *Zazděná*

  Walled In

  Ballad for alto and chamber ensemble set on lyrics by Karel Jaromír Erben.

  Lost music for an unachieved film project by Trnka.

From *Bajaja* (*Prince Bajaja*, 1950)
1950

- *Bajaja*

  Bajaja

  Songs for children soloists, children's choir, and piano.

1951

- *Princ Bajaja*

Prince Bajaja

Suite for orchestra and children's choir.

1970

- *Princ Bajaja*

  Prince Bajaja

  Suite for violin, guitar, and accordion.

1971

- *Princ Bajaja*

  Prince Bajaja

  Suite for flute, violin, viola, cello, and harp.

1972

- *Princ Bajaja. Vítězný pochod*

  Prince Bajaja. The Victory March

  For orchestra.

1979

- *Nonetto favoloso*

  Nonetto favoloso

  Suite for flute, oboe, clarinet, bassoon, French horn, violin, viola, cello, and contrabass.

1980

- *Princ Bajaja*

  Prince Bajaja

  Suite for accordion and electrophonic accordion.

1986

- *Princ Bajaja*

  Prince Bajaja

  Ballet from the film score, for orchestra.

  Libretto by Daniel Wiesner. Posthumously completed by Jan Klusák with own compositions and music from the film *The Czech Year.*

From *Veselý cirkus* (*The Merry Circus*, 1951)

1960

- *Veselý cirkus*

  The Merry Circus

  Suite for accordion and chamber ensemble.

  Compiled by Milan Bláha with the composer's permission.

1980

- *Cirkusová suita*

  Circus Suite

  For accordion and electrophonic accordion.

  Compiled by Milan Bláha with the composer's permission.

From *Dobrý voják Švejk* (*The Good Soldier Švejk* 1954–1955)

1954

- *Radecký mars*

  Radetzky March

  By Johann Strauss I; arranged for wind band.

From *Kuťásek a Kutilka jak ráno vstávali* (K uťásek
and Kutilka Woke up in the Morning, 1955)

1955

- *Loutkové scény*

  Puppet scenes

  Suite for accordion and orchestra.

  Compiled by Milan Bláha with the composer's permission.
  It later became part of the *Pohádky pro akordeon a orchestr*
  (*Fairy Tales for Accordion and Orchestra*, 1959).

From *Sen noci svatojánské* (*A Midsummer
Night's Dream*, 1959)

1959

- *Sen noci svatojánské*

  A Midsummer Night's Dream

  Prelude for orchestra.

- *Zamilovaná Titanie*

  Titania in Love

  For orchestra.

1961

- *Sen noci svatojánské*

  A Midsummer Night's Dream

  For piano and *ad libitum* singing voices.

  Arranged by Milan Šolc.

1966

- *Sen noci svatojánské*

  A Midsummer Night's Dream

  Suite for orchestra.

1972

- *Shakespearův úsměv*

  Shakespeare's Smile

  Six scenes for large orchestra.

  Parts 2–6 are from the film music, or add new material over that music.

1978

- *Sen noci svatojánské*

  A Midsummer Night's Dream

  Suite for orchestra.

1984

- *Sen noci svatojánské*

  A Midsummer Night's Dream

  Pantomime-ballet for orchestra.

  Libretto by Václav Trojan and Alena Hoblová.

References

Alberti, W. 1957. *Il cinema di animazione –1932–1956*. Torino: ERI.

Allan, R. 1999. *Walt Disney and Europe*. New Barnet: John Libbey.

Augustin, L. H. 2002. *Jiří Trnka*. Praha: Academia.

Bellano, M. 2013. Silent Strategies. Audiovisual Functions of the Music for Silent Cinema. *Kieler Beiträge zur Filmmusikforschung no. 9.* http://www.filmmusik.uni-kiel.de/KB9/KB9-Bellano.pdf (accessed February 26, 2019).

Bellano, M., Ricci, G., and Vanelli, M. 2013. *Animazione in cento film*. Recco: Le Mani.

Bendazzi, G. 1994. *Cartoons. One Hundred Years of Cinema Animation*. London: John Libbey.

Bendazzi, G. 2004. Defining Animation – A Proposal. http://www.giannalbertobendazzi.com/Content/resources/pdf/Animation-Essays/Defining_Animation-Giannalberto_Bendazzi2004.pdf (accessed July 14, 2018).

Bendazzi, G. 2015. *Animation: A World History*, 3 vols. Boca Raton, FL: CRC Press.

Bendazzi, G. 2017. *Twice the First: Quirino Cristiani and the Animated Feature Film*. Boca Raton, FL: CRC Press.

Bendazzi, G., Cecconello, M., and Michelone, G. 1995. *Coloriture. Voci, rumori, musiche nel cinema d'animazione*. Bologna: Pendragon.

Benešova, M. 1961. *Od špalíčku ke snu noci svatojanské*. Praha: Orbis.

Benešova, M. 1975. *Jiří Trnka: Rétrospective*. Montréal: La Cinémathèque québécoise.

Benešova, M. 2009. *Břetislav Pojar. Monograph of One of the Greatest Directors of Czech Animated Films*. Praha: Animation People.

Benešova, M., Berthomé, J. P., Delbonnel, B. et al. 1981. *Jiří Trnka. Fantasmagorie. Revue du film d'animation* nouvelle série no. 5.

Boček, J. 1965. *Jiří Trnka: Artist and Puppet Master*. London: Artia.

Bogatyrëv, P. G. 1980. *Il teatro di marionette*. Translated by Maria Di Salvo. Brescia: Grafo Edizioni.

Boillat, J. M. 1974. Jiří Trnka: 1912–1969. *Anthologie du Cinéma*, vol. VIII, no. 79; supplement to *L'Avant-Scène du Cinéma*, no. 149–150. Paris: Avant-Scène du Cinéma.

Bor, V., and Lucký, Š. 1958. *Trojan – filmová hudba*. Praha: SNKLHU.

Brode, D. 2000. *Shakespeare in the Movies: From the Silent Era to Shakespeare in Love*. Oxford: Oxford University Press.

Broz, J. 1952. Sul minuscolo palcoscenico vecchie leggende con pupazzi. *Cinema*, VIII(90): 18.

Caccamo, F., Helan, P., and Tria, M. 2011. *Primavera di Praga, risveglio europeo*. Firenze: Firenze University Press.

Casiraghi, U. 1951. *Cinema cecoslovacco ieri e oggi*. Roma: Edizioni dell'Ateneo.

Česálková, L., ed. 2017. *Czech Cinema Revisited: Politics, Aesthetics, Genres and Techniques*. Praha: National Film Archive.

Chattopadhyay, B. 2017. Reconstructing Atmospheres: Ambient Sound in Film and Media Production. https://journals.sagepub.com/doi/full/10.1177/2057047317742171 (accessed March 28, 2019).

Chion, M. 1982. *La voix au cinéma*. Paris: Éditions de l'étoile.

Chion, M. 2001. *L'audiovisione. Suono e immagine nel cinema*. Translated by Dario Buzzolan. Torino: Lindau.

Chvojková, H. 1990. *Jiří Trnka*. Plzeň: Západočeské nakladatelství.

Clementi, M. 2007. *Cecoslovacchia*. Milano: Unicopli.

Coyle, R., ed. 2010. *Drawn to Sound. Animation Film Music and Sonicity*. London: Equinox.

Crafton, D. 1993. *Before Mickey. The Animated Film*, pp. 1898–1928. Chicago, IL: The University of Chicago Press.

Crescenzi, B. 1953a. I pupazzi cecoslovacchi. I – Cenni e precedenti storici. *L'eco del cinema e dello spettacolo*, 50: 7–8.

Crescenzi, B. 1953b. I pupazzi cecoslovacchi. II – Negli studi di Gottwaldow. *L'eco del cinema e dello spettacolo*, 51: 7, 10.

Crescenzi, B. 1953c. I pupazzi cecoslovacchi. III – Negli studi di Praga e di Brno. *L'eco del cinema e dello spettacolo*, 52: 7, 10.

Crescenzi, B. 1953d. I pupazzi cecoslovacchi. IV – Pupi e no. *L'eco del cinema e dello spettacolo*, 53: 7, 10.

Cuenca, C. F. 1965. *Jiří Trnka*. Madrid: Filmoteca Nacional de España.

Deke, R. F. 1951. The Emperor's Nightingale. *Film Music Notes*, 10(6): 8–9.

Dohnalová, L., ed. 2005. *Czech Music*. Praha: Theatre Institute.

Dutka, E. 2000. Jiří Trnka: Walt Disney of the East! http://www.awn. com/animationworld/jiri-trnka-walt-disney-east (accessed July 12, 2018).

Falvey, Ch. 2009. Studio Bratři v Triku – The cradle of Czech Animation. http://www.radio.cz/en/section/arts/studio-bratri-v-triku-the-cradle-of-czech-animation (accessed July 12, 2018).

Fazio, M. 2003. *Lo specchio, il gioco e l'estasi. La regia teatrale in Germania dai Meininger a Jessner (1874–1933)*. Roma: Bulzoni.

Flašar, M. 2013. Jan Novák, Jiří Trnka a Jejich Kibernetická Babička. *Musicologica Brunensia*, 48: 57–61. https://digilib.phil.muni. cz/bitstream/handle/11222.digilib/128914/1_Musicologica Brunensia_48-2013-1_8.pdf?sequence=1 (accessed July 12, 2018).

Ford, Ch., and Hammond, R. 2015. *Polish Film. A Twentieth Century History*. Jefferson, MI: McFarland.

Fornaro, P. 2004. *La tentazione autoritaria: istituzioni, politica e società nell'Europa centro-orientale tra le due guerre mondiali*. Messina: Rubbettino Editore.

Fraňková, R. 2011. Jiří Trnka: An Artist Who Turned Puppets into Film Stars. http://www.radio.cz/en/section/czech-history/jiri-trnka-an-artist-who-turned-puppets-into-film-stars (accessed July 12, 2018).

Furniss, M. 1998. *Art in Motion: Animation Aesthetics*. New Barnet: John Libbey.

Goldmark, D. 2005. *Tunes for 'Toons. Music and the Hollywood Cartoon*. Berkeley, CA: University of California Press.

Gregorová, J. 2007. Hermína Týrlová. http://www.radio.cz/fr/rubrique/ celebres/hermina-tyrlova (accessed July 12, 2018).

Grym, P. 1988. *Klauni v dřevacich*. Praha: Merkur.

Gunning, T. 1990. The Cinema of Attractions: Early Film, Its Spectator, and the Avant-Garde. In T. Elsaesser (ed.) *Early Cinema: Space, Frame, Narrative*, pp. 56–62. London: BFI.

Hames, P. 2009. *Czech and Slovak Cinema. Theme and Tradition*. Edinburgh: Edinburgh University Press.

Hanslick, E. 1974. *The Beautiful in Music*. Translated By Gustav Cohen. Cambridge: Da Capo Press.

Hašek, J. 2016. *Le avventure del bravo soldato Švejk nella Grande Guerra*. Translated by Annalisa Cosentino. Milano: Mondadori.

Hepner, A. 1951. The Emperor's Nightingale. *Film Music Notes*, 10(5): 7–8.

Horáková, P. 2003. Forced Displacement of Czech Population under Nazis in 1938 and 1943. http://www.radio.cz/en/section/talking/forced-displacement-of-czech-population-under-nazis-in-1938-and-1943 (accessed July 12, 2018).

Hořejši, J., and Struska, J., 1969. *Occhio magico – Il cinema d'animazione cecoslovacco 1944–1969*. Praha: Filmexport.

Hronková, L. 2014. Geneze baletu Oskara Nedbala Z Pohádky do Pohádky v korespondenci uložené v divadelním oddělení národního muzea. *Acta Musei Nationalis Pragae Series A – Historia*, 68(3–4): 47–54.

Hrubín, F., Skupová, J., Sklenář, Z. et al. 1971. *Jiří Trnka*. Praha: Československý spisovatel.

Hurtová, J. 2010. *AFIT 1941–1944 (1948). Inventář*. Praha: Národní filmový archiv. http://nfa.cz/wp-content/uploads/2014/12/AFIT.pdf (accessed February 5, 2019).

Jirásek, P. 2015. Josef Skupa: The Birth of a Modern Artist. *Theatralia*, 18(2): 168–230. https://digilib.phil.muni.cz/handle/11222.digilib/134425 (accessed July 12, 2018).

Jiráskova, M., and Jirásek, P. 2011. *Loutka a moderna*. Praha: JAMU.

Johnston, R. 2011. Josef Lada – Landscape Painter and Švejk Illustrator. http://www.radio.cz/en/section/czech-history/josef-lada-landscape-painter-and-svejk-illustrator (accessed July 12, 2018).

Jůn, D. 2012. Jiří Trnka: 100th Anniversary of the Birth of a Great Czech Animator. http://www.radio.cz/en/section/czech-history/jiri-trnka-100th-anniversary-of-the-birth-of-a-great-czech-animator (accessed July 12, 2018).

Jůn, D. 2015. 70th Anniversary Special – The Czech Resistance During. *World War II*. http://www.radio.cz/en/section/special/70th-anniversary-special-the-czech-resistance-during-world-war-ii (accessed July 12, 2018).

Kačor, M., Podhradský, M., and Mertová, M. 2010. *Zlatý věck česke loutkové animace*. Praha: Animation People and Mladá fronta.

Kenety, B. 2005. The 17th of November: Remembering Jan Opletal, martyr of an occupied nation. http://www.radio.cz/en/section/panorama/the-17th-of-november-remembering-jan-opletal-martyr-of-an-occupied-nation (accessed July 12, 2018).

Kouba, J, and Volek, T. 1990. *A Historical Survey of Czech Music 2*. https://is.muni.cz/el/1490/podzim2009/CZS33/8974387/lecture4/ (accessed February 8, 2019).

Koutek, J. 1965. *Quinta colonna all'Est. I nazisti nei Sudeti (1933–1938)*. Anonymous translation. Roma: Editori Riuniti.

Large, B. 1970. *Smetana*. London: Duckworth.

Laura, E. G. 1960. *Il film cecoslovacco*. Roma: Edizioni dell'Ateneo.

Liehm, M., and Liehm, A. J. 1977. *The Most Important Art: Eastern European Film After 1945*. Berkeley and Los Angeles, CA: University of California Press.

Lord, P., and Sibley, B. 2015. *Cracking Animation. The Aardman Book of 3-D Animation*. London: Thames & Hudson.

Máchal, J. 1995. *Bájesloví slovanské*. Olomouc: Votobia.

Marker, Ch. 1952. Prince Bajaja de Jiří Trnka, une forme d'ornament. *Les Cahiers du Cinéma*, 8. http://chrismarker.org/chris-marker/prince-bayaya-de-jiri-trnka-une-forme-dornement/ (accessed July 12, 2018).

Martin, A. 1960a. Pour qui sont ces Trnka? I. *Cahiers du Cinéma*, 104: 31–42.

Martin, A. 1960b. Pour qui sont ces Trnka? II. *Cahiers du Cinéma*, 105: 22–34.

Martin, A. 1960c. Pour qui sont ces Trnka? III. *Cahiers du Cinéma*, 107: 28–39.

McCormick, J., and Pratasik, B. 1998. *Popular puppet theatre in Europe, 1800 - 1914*. Cambridge: Cambridge University Press.

Miceli, S. 2009. Musica per Film. *Storia, Estetica, Analisi, Tipologie*. Milano: Ricordi LIM.

Michelone, G., and Valenzise, G. 1998. *Bibidi bobidi bu: la musica nei cartoni animati da Betty Boop a Peter Gabriel*. Roma: Castelvecchi.

Montroni, G. 2011. Scenari del mondo contemporaneo dal 1815 a oggi. Bari: Laterza, Bari.

Munroe, C. 2010. The Passing of a Puppet Master: Kihachiro Kawamoto (1925–2010). http://nishikataeiga.blogspot.it/2010/08/passing-of-puppet-master-kihachiro.html (accessed July 12, 2018).

Parrott, C. 1982. *Jaroslav Hašek: A Study of Švejk and the Short Stories*. Cambridge: Cambridge University Press.

Pek, A. 1953. Trojanova hudba v Trnkových loutkových filmech. *Film a doba, year IV*, 5: 621.

Piccoli, M. T. 1948. Cinema di stato a Praga e Varsavia. *Cinema*, 3: 73–75.

Pilka, J., and Matzner, A. 2002. *Česká filmová hudba*. Praha: Dauphin.

Pilková, Z. 1988. Eighteenth Century Folk Music in the Czech Lands: Comments on the State of Research. In M. Beckermann and G. Bauer (eds) *Janáček and Czech Music. Proceedings of The International Conference*, Saint Louis, pp. 155–164. Stuyvesant, NY: Pendragon Press.

Polt, H. R. 1964. The Czeckoslovak Animated Film. *Film Quarterly*, 17(3): 31–40.

Purves, B. J. C. 2015. *Animazione stop motion*. Translated by Federico Taibi. Modena: Logos.

Raifanda, Z. 1957. Skupův Spejbl. *Československy loutkař*, 7: 2, 31.

Randel, D. M. 1978. *The Harvard Concise Dictionary of Music and Musicians*. Cambridge: Harvard University Press.

Redi, R. 1999. Cinema muto italiano (1896–1930). Roma: Bianco & Nero.

Richter, H. 1952. Easel-Scroll-Film. *Magazine of Art*, 45: 78–86.

Richter, J. 2011. The Film Score Genius Zdeněk Liška. http://www.radio.cz/en/section/panorama/the-film-score-genius-zdenek-liska (accessed July 12, 2018).

Rondolino, G. 2003. *Storia del cinema d'animazione*. Torino: Einaudi.

Rosenblum, S. P. 1994. The Uses of Rubato in Music, Eighteenth to Twentieth Centuries. *Performance Practice Review*, 7(1): 33–53.

Sayer, D. 2000. *The Coasts of Bohemia: A Czech History*. Princeton, NJ: Princeton University Press.

Selby, A. 2013. *Animation*. London: Laurence King.

Servant, C. 2009. Les Vieilles Légendes tchèques: un traitement cinématographique par Jiří Trnka au début des années 1950. http://www.inalco.fr/sites/default/files/asset/document/servant_cinema_animation_2009_2.pdf. (accessed July 12, 2018).

Šímová, V. 2010. Film Music in Czech Music Periodicals in the 1960s. *Musicologica Olomucensia*, 11: 87–94.

Suchenski, R. 2009. Hans Richter. http://sensesofcinema.com/2009/great-directors/hans-richter/ (accessed July 13, 2018).

Štěpánek, V., and Karásek, B. 1964. *Breve storia della musica cèca e slovacca. Parte prima. La musica cèca*. Praha: Orbis.

Stravinsky, I. 1962. *An Autobiography*. Tranlated by anonymous. New York: W. W: Norton.

Strusková, E. 2013. *The Dodals: Pioneers of Czech Animated Film*. Praha: National Film Archive.

Tetiva, V. 1999. *Jiří Trnka (1912–1969)*. Praha: Alšova jihočeská galerie v Hluboké nad Vltavou.

Thomas, F., and Johnston, O. 1981. *The Illusion of Life: Disney Animation*. New York: Disney Editions.

Trnková, R. 1972. *Muj syn*. Praha: Československý spisovatel.

Velinger, J. 2011. First Part of Czech Classic the Good Soldier Švejk Published 90 Years Ago. http://www.radio.cz/en/section/currafrs/first-part-of-czech-classic-the-good-soldier-svejk-published-90-years-ago (accessed July 12, 2018).

Vičar, J. 1986. Nástin života a periodizace tvorby Václava Trojana. *Zivá hudba*, 9: 273–288.

Vičar, J. 1989. *Václav Trojan*. Praha: Panton.

Vičar, J. 2005. *Imprints. Essays on Czech Music and Aesthetics*. Olomouc and Praha: Palacký University and Togga.

Vonderková, I. 2006. Josef Skupa. http://www.radio.cz/es/rubrica/personalidades/josef-skupa-1 (accessed July 12, 2018).

White, T. 2013. *Animation from Pencils to Pixels*. New York and London: Focal Press.

Williams, R. 2015. *The Animator's Survival Kit*. London: Faber & Faber.

Willoughby, I. 2014. Karel Zeman's Work Inspirational, Says Director Tim Burton on Eve of Prague Art Show. http://www.radio.cz/en/section/curraffrs/karel-zemans-work-inspirational-says-director-tim-burton-on-eve-of-prague-art-show (accessed July 12, 2018).

Zanotto, P. 1969. *Vecchie leggende ceche: un film di Jiří Trnka*. Padova: Radar.

Zapletal, M. 2015. *V mezích socialistického realismu i proti nim. Trojanova hudba ke Starým pověstem českým*. Praha: Národní filmový archiv.

Index

Printed in the United States
by Baker & Taylor Publisher Services